I0519351

Septuagint:

Judith

Septuagint, Volume 12

SCRIPTURAL RESEARCH INSTITUTE
Published by Digital Ink Productions, 2024

Copyright

Septuagint: Judith

Second edition. March 6, 2024

Copyright © 2024 Scriptural Research Institute

ISBN: 978-1-998288-58-8

The Septuagint was translated into Greek at the Library of Alexandria between 250 and 132 BC.

This English translation was created by the Scriptural Research Institute in 2019 through 2021, primarily from the Codex Vaticanus, although the Codex Alexandrinus was also used for reference. Additionally, the Hebrew translations of the Book of Judith were used for comparative analysis.

The image used for the cover is an artistic reinterpretation of 'Judith and Holofernes' by Michelangelo Merisi da Caravaggio, painted between 1598 and 1602. The original painting is currently on display in the Galleria Nazionale d'Arte Antica, in Rome.

Table of Contents

TABLE OF CONTENTS

TABLE OF CONTENTS

Forward

In the mid 3rd century BC, King Ptolemy II Philadelphus of Egypt ordered a translation of the ancient Hebrew scriptures for the Library of Alexandria, which resulted in the creation of the Septuagint. The original version, published circa 250 BC, only included the Torah, or in Greek terms, the Pentateuch. The Torah is the five books traditionally credited to Moses, circa 1500 BC: Cosmic Genesis, Exodus, Leviticus, Numbers, and Deuteronomy. According to Jewish tradition, the original Torah was lost when the Babylonians destroyed the Temple of Solomon and was later rewritten by Ezra the Scribe from memory during the Second Temple period.

It is generally accepted that there were several versions of the ancient Hebrew and Samaritan scriptures before the translation of the Septuagint, mostly written in Canaanite or Aramaic, although the older sections of the Torah appear to have originated in Akkadian Cuneiform. The origin of the Book of Judith has been debated for thousands of years, and is often assumed to have been written in Greek as anti-Hellenic propaganda during the Maccabean Revolt. It isn't clear why an anti-Hellenic book would have been written in Greek by an Aramaic-speaking people, yet, no ancient copies of it survive in Hebrew, Aramaic, or Phoenician (Samaritan / Judahite). There are Hebrew translations, however, they are dated to the middle ages, 1000 years after the oldest surviving copies of the Judith found in the Septuagint. The Greek translations are remarkably consistent compared to the radically different versions of the Book of Tobit in the surviving copies of the Septuagint.

The Hebrew versions of Judith are not consistent, as there are two known versions, one virtually identical to the Greek, and another shorter version. The reason the book of Judith is often considered to be anti-Greek propaganda, is derived from analysis of the Hebrew versions, in which the king has a different name from the Greek version. In the Greek version, the name of the king is Nebuchadnezzar, while in the Hebrew version his name is Antiochus, which is accepted as a reference to Antiochus IV Epiphanes, the King of the Seleucid Empire between 175 and 164 BC, when the Maccabean Revolt was taking place. Conversely, in the Greek version, Nebuchadnezzar is referred to as the king of Assyria, however, Assyria never had a king named Nebuchadnezzar, which is generally accepted as proof that the name Nebuchadnezzar was substituted for another name. This naturally leads to the conclusion that the name Antiochus was replaced with Nebuchadnezzar by the scribes at the library of Alexandria, in order to obscure the origin of the book as a piece of anti-Greek propaganda.

That the Maccabees fought the rule of Antiochus IV is not in doubt. That the Hebrew version of Judith is anti-Hellenic is not in doubt. However, all versions include elements inconsistent with the reign of Antiochus, which either have to be dismissed as fiction, or treated as indicators that he was not the original king in the book. The most obvious inconsistency is the reference to a general revolt across most of his empire in his 17th year. There was no general revolt during Antiochus reign, and he only ruled for 11 years. There is a story about him invading Media and the king of the Medes being killed in combat, yet, in Antiochus' era, there was neither a king of the Medes, nor even a kingdom of the Medes, as the Medes had been assimilated into the Persian population centuries earlier, and their historic lands were part of his empire. There is the even more stunning anachronism of him fighting a war against Elam, which had been basically destroyed by the Assyrians 500 years earlier, and recolonized by Persians. In Antiochus' era, the land that had once been Elam, was part of Persia, which was part of his empire as well, and there simply were no Elamites to go to war against.

In short, the political geography of the book is either complete nonsense and the author knew nothing of the world he or she lived in, or the book dates to a different era, and the anti-Hellenic version of it was created as a piece of propaganda, likely during the Maccabean Revolt. The name of the king in the book of Judith is named Nebuchadnezzar (Ναβουχοδονοσορ), which was the name of the king of Babylon, between 605 and 562 BC. However, other than the name of the king, no other elements of the story indicate the story originated with the Babylonians. Nebuchadnezzar did not fight the Medes, and could not have killed the king of Media, as the two countries were close allies at the time, and under King Cyaxares the Median Empire reached its peak. Nebuchadnezzar didn't launch a war against the Elamites, who in fact fell under the control of Cyaxares's Median Empire. As the name Nebuchadnezzar was used to replace Achiacharos (Αχιαχαρος) in the book of Tobit, when the Sinaiticus version was simplified into the Vaticanus version, it's likely that the name Nebuchadnezzar was simply used to replace an older name as well.

There are several indicators in the book that point to the original king being Ashurbanipal, the king of Assyria between 668 and 627 BC. Ashurbanipal did fight two wars against Elam, and virtually annihilated the Elamites in the second war. Ashurbanipal also invaded Media, and during the fighting the Median king Phraortes was killed, allowing Ashurbanipal to claim victory, even though he didn't consolidate his victory and integrate Media back into the Assyrian Empire. When Ashurbanipal had launched the invasion of Media, in his 17th year, he ordered the local kings from across his empire to send troops to the war, but almost all refused, which was a general insurrection. Therefore, while committed to the war against Media, after defeating the Medians, he was eager to return to Assyria, and restore order to his empire.

All of these major points regarding the similarity of Ashurbanipal to the king in the Book of Judith correlate, and have been noted for centuries, however, there are still a few inconsistencies in the geographical details, that do not support either king's reign, and in fact, can not be synchronized with any known king that lived. One of these inconsistencies is the reference to Phoud (Φουδ) being en route to Loud (Λουδ) from Cilicia, during the march of the Assyrian army. Loud was the Greek translation of Lud (לוּד), which was the Hebrew name of Lydia, a kingdom that dominated western Anatolia in the 7th century BC. However, Phoud was a Greek transliteration of the Hebrew Put (פוּט), which was a name for Cyrene under Persian rule.

One would not march an army from Cilicia, in southeast Anatolia, to Lydia, in western Anatolia, via Cyrene in North Africa, but through Phrygia, in Central Anatolia. The Kingdom of Phrygia ruled central Anatolia in the 8th century BC, however, was devastated by the

Cimmerians from the territory of modern Ukraine and southern Russia circa 676 BC, who then occupied the land and used it as a base to attack the neighboring nations, including the kingdom of Lydia. Early in the reign of the Assyrian King Ashurbanipal, the kingdom of Lydia made formal contact with the Assyrians, and requested assistance fighting the Cimmerians. Ashurbanipal sent his army west to defeat the Cimmerians, and free the Lydians. He is the only Assyrian king recorded to have ever sent an army to Lydia, however, it passed through Phrygia, not Cyrene.

The land of Phrygia became part of Lydia after the Lydians finally conquered the Cimmerians in 620 BC, and later fell under the rule of the Medians and then Persians. The name had apparently lost its geographical location over time, as in addition to the satrapy (province) Greater Phrygia, which was located where the ancient kingdom was, the Persians named the satrapy in northwest Anatolia Lesser Phrygia. If the original text was written in the 7th century BC, then the name that the Samaritans would have used for Phrygia is unknown today, and possibly wasn't known 2200 years ago at the Library of Alexandria as well, which resulted in the mistransliteration of Phoud.

The Book of Judith also includes the curious reference to the river Hydaspes (Ὑδάσπην), which is accepted as the ancient Greek name of the Jhelum River in modern northern Pakistan. The river is mentioned as one of the places that were rebelling at the time against the king, however, the Assyrian Empire did not extend to Pakistan. The Hydaspes was famous during the Greek era, as a site of a major battle between Alexander the Great's armies and the Indian army led by King Porus (Πῶρος), who was killed in battle. This is one of the indicators used to prove the book originated in the Greek era, however, it is equally possible that the Greeks did not recognize an Aramaic name and replaced it with a similar-sounding Greek name.

If the name of a Mesopotamian river was replaced, it was most likely the name Harpasos (Ἅρπασος), which is believed to have been the early Greek name for the Karasu River in modern Turkey or the Çoruh River in modern Turkey and Georgia. Sometime after the conquest of Alexander, the Karasu was renamed Têleboas (Τηλεβόας), and the Çoruh was renamed the Acampsis (Ἄκαμψις). However, in Xenophon's Anabasis, written between 401 and 354 BC, he referred to a river in the region as the Harpasos. In Anabasis, Xenophon recounted the march of the Greek mercenary forces into Persian-held Anatolia in 401 BC, hired by the Persian prince Cyrus the Younger, who was attempting to usurp the throne from his brother Artaxerxes II. It is not clear which river he was referencing, however, based on the path the Greeks took through Anatolia, scholars believe it was either the Karasu or the Çoruh. The Karasu is a long river in eastern modern Turkey that flows into the Euphrates, and was within the Assyrian Empire, while the Çoruh is a fast-flowing river in modern northeast Turkey and Georgia, which flows into the Black Sea and was not under the control of the Assyrian Empire, therefore, the reference would have likely been to the Karasu.

The name Harpasos itself, regardless of which river it applied to, was a Greek transliteration of the local name of the river, which had been lost by the time the Library of Alexandria translated Judith, however, if Judith was originally written during the Assyrian, Median, or Persian eras, the text would have been written in Aramaic or Akkadian Cuneiform, both of which would have used the original name of the river, not the later Greek name. This means that the Greeks would not have known which river the name applied to in their language, and seem to have substituted a famous and similarly named Greek river. While this substitution of Harpasos with Hydaspes is entirely theoretical, it certainly makes more sense than the inclusion of Indian armies with the Mesopotamian armies in the era before the rise of the Persian Empire. This, however, does require the text to date back to the Assyrian, Median, or Persian eras, which therefore also requires several substitutions to have taken place throughout the text.

The Book of Judith contains some very unusual spelling of town names in Judah and Canaan, which makes it unlikely the book was written in Hebrew. One example is the town of Bethany, which is spelled Bêthania (Βηθανία) in the Gospels, but Batanê (Βατανη) in the Book of Judith. The version in Judith appears to be a transliteration into Greek of the Aramaic name Byt Ônyå (ܐ‎^‎ܝ‎ܥ ܢ‎^‎ܥ), while the version in the Gospels is clearly derived from the later Hebrew Byt Ôny (בית עני). The Hebrew and Aramaic names are very similar, and mean almost the same thing, however, the name of the town in Judith does appear to have been transliterated from an Aramaic text.

Another Aramaic or Hebrew word also appears to have been transliterated directly in Greek: Cheleôn (Χελεων) from the Semitic term kôlywn (כעליון), which translates approximately as 'the capital' or 'of the chief.' The word is generally transliterated directly as a name of a settlement, or a people, however, no known settlement or group used this name. The Book of Judith also has the strange word Abrôna (Αβρωνα), which is often treated as a proper name of a town along the Eurphrates, but does not match any known town in the region. The

word does not appear to be a proper name, but a transliteration of the Assyrian word ebēru (𒂊𒁉), which translates as 'to cross.' This suggests the Book of Judith was
translated into Assyrian cuneiform, which was the official script of the Neo-Assyrian Empire, and used alongside Aramaic in the Neo-Babylonian Empire. If so, it
must have been written before the Neo-Babylonian
Empire fell to the Persians, in 539 BC. Based on the
described movements of the army, this appears to be the
only rational translation of the texts, as they started in
the Arabian Desert, following which they crossed the
Euphrates, and then 'Abrona' following which they
were back at the Mediterranean Sea at Cilicia. Therefore
the Akkadian term is restored in this translation.

Another strange spelling found in the Book of Judith
is the name Okina (Οκινα), which is generally accepted
as being a reference to Acre, a port city on the modern
Israeli Mediterranean coast. The spelling of the name is
odd because the Greeks generally spelled it as Acra
(Ἀκρα) or Acê (Ἀκη), which is similar to the Egyptian
Ôkå (𓂝𓎡𓅱), Neo-Babylonian Ak^{ki} (𒀀𒆗), Phoenician Ôk (𐤏𐤊), and Hebrew Akkô (עַכּוֹ). The location of
Okina, along the coast between Tyre and Yavne indicates it was a reference to Acre. The spelling of the name
suggests that it was a transliteration error during a translation from Canaanite to Aramaic, where a Canaanite R

(𐤉) was replaced with an Aramaic N (𐤍), which indicates the book started in Judahite or Samaritan before being translated into Aramaic.

The Book of Judith also includes two references to Tyre in the list of names the Assyrians conquered along the coast, listing it both as Tyrô (Τύρῳ) and Shur (Σουρ). Sur (صور) was, and still is, the local name for Tyre, which was mentioned in the text directly before Sur. The English name Tyre is derived from the Greek name Týros (Τύρος), which was in use by the Greeks since at least the 5ᵗʰ century BC. The local Phoenician name was Sr (𐤑𐤓), which meant 'rocks,' as there was a rocky harbor there, with a rocky island off the shore.

At the time the story is set, the island and coastal town were two settlements under a common government, both called Sur. The island had originally tried to remain independent when the Assyrians conquered the coastal city, relying on Tyre's distant colonies in North Africa to sustain it, however, once the Assyrians built a Mediterranean fleet, the island had surrendered to Assyria. The inclusion of the second reference to Tyre/Sr is therefore valid in the era, and seems to be absolute proof that the original Book of Judith predates Alexander the Great constructing a causeway out to the island in order to conquer it. Since Alexander's time, the two settlements have been one town, and there would have been no reason to mention them separately.

Unfortunately, even though the majority of the anachronisms can be explained by placing the story in the time of King Ashurbanipal of Assyria, there is no surviving copy of the text to prove that it was originally written with him in it. The massive number of anachronisms do make the surviving texts read as fiction in a nonsense world, which then results in the text losing any historical merit. All surviving Greek copies of Judith are essentially the same. While the Hebrew copies similar to the Greek versions, but refer to Antiochus instead of Nebuchadnezzar, this is equally nonsensical as it now refers to Antiochus fighting wars against kingdoms that had not existed for 500 years. Therefore two versions are included in this translation. The first is a translation of the Septuagint's Judith, including the anachronistic names, while the second is a historical restoration that used the name Ashurbanipal instead of Nebuchadnezzar, and corrects other anachronisms as much as possible. In both versions there are still references to unknown places and peoples, however, after 2700 years, it does seem likely that there would be.

It is also worth noting that while the Hebrew version is often accepted, especially by Jews, as a fictional story that was promoted by the Maccabees as propaganda against the Greeks, and the Hebrew variant may have started that way, it nevertheless could not have been popular in Judea, as no fragments of it have yet been identified among the Dead Sea Scrolls. It also could not have been popular several centuries later when the Masorites began copying the Hebrew and Aramaic texts that ultimately formed the Masoretic Texts, as they did not include it. Jewish interest in the story appears to have originated in the Medieval Era, which is the earliest the Hebrew versions can be dated to, and they may have simply been translated from the Greek or Syriac versions used by Christians. If so, the anachronism of Antiochus' name wouldn't even be a consideration when attempting to understand the origin of the text.

The Septuagint is generally considered to have reached its current form, not counting later redactions, about 132 BC. Therefore, if the Greek version is based on a Hebrew or Aramaic fictional text written during the Maccabean Revolt, it was basically new, as the Maccabean Revolt was between 165 and 140 BC. If the author was contemporary with the translators at the Library, then the number of oddly spelled names, and misplaced rivers, simply does not make sense. The name of Acre was standardized by that time.

The book of Judith also has the names of the Mishmar (משמר / Μοχμουρ) and Michmas (מכמש) rivers mixed

up, which is very strong evidence that text was translated at the Library sometime between 161 and 143 BC,
when the Greeks still viewed the Maccabees as terrorists.
The book described the area of the Michmas (מכמש)
river, northeast of Jerusalem in what was Assyrian-occu-
pied Samaria at the time. The geography is clear, and the
river was along the Assyrian king Sennacherib's route
when he invaded Samaria a few decades before the
insurrection during Ashurbanipal's reign, however, the
book uses the name Mishmar (משמר / Μοχμουρ), which
is an unrelated river southeast of Jerusalem. The reason
for this substitution by the translator, was most likely
because the Michmas was the base that Jason's armies
were using to attack the Greeks during the Maccabean
Revolt.

Neither a Greek nor Judean author in that era should
have mixed up the Mishmar (משמר / Μοχμουρ) and
Michmas (מכמש) rivers. Also any author that knew the
coast of Phoenicia and Judea well enough to name the
cities should not have named Tyre twice. Moreover, at
that point, almost the entire Septuagint would have been
translated, so why were names transliterated into Greek
in new and unusual ways? Overall, while the language
of the text is consistent with Koine Greek, the translation
seems out of place within the Septuagint, as if it was
independently translated, and then added to the collec-

tion, however, whatever its origin, it was likely translated during the Maccabean Revolt.

In 200 BC, the Greek Kingdom of Syria under the Seleucid Dynasty took Judea from Egypt, and began an effort to Hellenize the Judeans, and effectively banned traditional Judaism. This Hellenizing activity was partially successful, creating the Sadducee faction of Judaism, however, it also led to the Maccabean Revolt in 165 BC, which itself created the independent Kingdom of Judea. This Kingdom had a tenuous alliance with the Roman Republic until General Pompey conquered Syria into the Roman Republic in 69 BC. Pompey's goal was to liberate Greek-speaking communities in the Middle East that had fallen under the rule of non-Greeks when the Seleucids Syrian Empire had collapsed, and he carved up Judea, and Edom to the southeast, placing Greek-speaking cities under the protection of the Roman province of Syria. He also liberated several smaller communities that had been occupied by Judea, granting them self-government, including Ashdod, Yavne, Jaffa, Dora, Marissa, and Samaria.

A series of wars including both Julius Caesar's campaigns, and a Parthian invasion led to the weakening of the Hasmonean dynasty, and in 37 AD, the Roman Senate appointed Herod the Great as King of Judea. Herod's rule wasn't particularly popular, as he allowed the Romans to establish themselves within Judea, however, he did expand Judea, reintegrating the Greek and Samaritan cities, and annexing Galilee and Edom. When he died, his kingdom was divided between four successors, a situation that ended in 66 AD when the Romans conquered the region. An uprising in 120 AD led to the Jews being exiled from Judea, and the region became a Greco-Roman colony. In the wake of the Jews, the Samaritans rose in numbers, along with the Christians once Christianity was legalized. Between 529 and 555 AD, the Samaritans revolted and were effectively annihilated, by Constantinople the Eastern Roman capital.

Outside of Judea, the Septuagint was the dominant form of Jewish scriptures across the Greek-speaking world, which by the beginning of the Christian era extended from the Roman Empire in the west, to the Indo-Greek Kingdom in the east. Jewish traders had established small colonies along the trade routes of the Red Sea and the Indian Ocean, reaching as far south as Yemen, and as far east as southern India, and these Jews spoke Greek and used the Septuagint.

The earliest Christian Bibles, all used the Septuagint, however, by the 4th century some Christian scholars were debating whether they should retranslate the Old Testament from the version the Jews were using, and some even suggested using the Samaritan version. Both suggestions were generally dismissed as heretical, as Jesus and the Apostles had quoted from the Septuagint, even though they had access to the Hebrew version then in use. This argument held in the west until the Middle Ages, when Catholic Bibles switched to the Masoretic Texts. In the east, Orthodox Bibles continued to use the Septuagint, as they do today. To the south, the Ethiopian Tewahedo Church continued to use the Septuagint, and across Asia, the Thomas Christians and Nestorians continued to use the Septuagint.

Only in Western Europe were the later Masoretic Text adopted, abandoning the more ancient Septuagint, on the assumption that the Jews had copied their texts more faithfully than the Greeks had translated them. This assumption carried forward into the Protestant Churches that broke off from the Catholic Church, and therefore almost all Protestant Bibles use the Masoretic Texts for the basis of the Old Testament.

Unfortunately, this means that the earliest Christian writing is generally confusing and ignored by Protestants and Catholics. The earliest Christians of the first and second centuries quoted books that are no longer in the Bible, and as such, their writings are not always understood. Septuagint: Judith is a 21st century translation aimed at correcting this problem.

FORWARD

One of the problems with academic translations of the Septuagint, is the use of unfamiliar names or terms, as the Septuagint was written in Greek, and therefore many names are unrecognizable to modern English readers who are used to Hebrew-derived names. This project uses the more commonly understood Hebrew-derived names instead of their Greek translations, such as Canaan instead of Chanaan, and Melchizedek instead of Melchisedec. Common modern names are also used instead of either Greek or Hebrew terms when geographical locations are known, such as the archaeological name Uruk instead of the Greek Orech, or the Hebrew Erech, and the archaeological term Sumer instead of Shinar or Senar.

Judith: Chapter 1

In the twelfth year of the reign of Nebuchadnezzar,[1] who reigned from the great Assyrian city of Nineveh.[2] In the days of Arphaxad,[3] who ruled over the Medes[4] from Ecbatana,[5] he built stone cut walls around Ecbatana from stones three cubits wide and six cubits long. He made the height of the wall seventy cubits, and the width fifty cubits, and set the towers for the gates a hundred cubits high, and the width of the foundation sixty cubits. He made the gates that raised, seventy cubits high and forty cubits wide, for his mighty armies of infantry to go out through in formation.

In those days King Nebuchadnezzar declared war against King Arphaxad in the great plain, which is the plain in the region of Ray.[6] There came against him all those that lived in the hill country, and by the Euphrates, Tigris, and Jhelum[7] rivers, and from the plain of Uruk[8] the king of the Elamites,[9] and a great many nations of the Chaldeans,[10] assembled themselves to the battle.

Nebuchadnezzar, king of the Assyrians sent messengers to all that lived in Persia, and to all that lived to the west. To those that lived in Cilicia, Damascus, Lebanon, Anti-Lebanon, and to all that lived on the sea coast, to the nations of Carmel, Gilead, Galilee, and the great plain of Yizre'el,[11] to all that were in Samaria and the cities beyond the Jordan to Jerusalem, and Bethany,[12] Chelus, Kadesh, and the river of Egypt, and Tahpanhes,[13] and Ramesses,[14] and all the land of Goshen, beyond Tanis and Memphis, and to all the inhabitants of Egypt to the borders of Kush.[15] But all the inhabitants of the ignored the commandment of Nebuchadnezzar king of the Assyrians and they did not accompany him into the battle, as they were not afraid of him. He was viewed by them as standing alone, and they sent away his ambassadors in disgrace.

Therefore Nebuchadnezzar was very angry with all these countries, and swore by his throne and kingdom, that he would certainly be avenged on all the lands of Cilicia, Damascus, and Syria, and that he would kill with the sword all the inhabitants of the land of Moab, Amman, Judah, Egypt, to the borders of the two seas. He marched in battle formation with his strength against King Arphaxad in the seventeenth year,[16] and he defeated him in battle, and he overthrew the power of Arphaxad, and all his cavalry, and all his chariots. He became lord of his cities, and traveled to Ecbatana, and captured the towers, and spoiled the streets, and turned its beauty into shame. He also captured Arphaxad in the mountains of Ray, and pierced him with his darts, and destroyed him completely that day. Afterward, he returned to Nineveh, with his company of sundry nations, a great multitude of soldiers, and he relaxed and celebrated, both he and his army for a hundred and twenty days.

Judith: Chapter 1 Notes

1 Codex Vaticanus: Nabouchodonosor
(ΝΑΒΟΥΧΟΔΟΝΟΣΟΡ)

There was no known Assyrian king named Nebuchadnezzar. It is believed by most scholars that this is a cryptic reference to the Seleucid Dynasty king named Antiochus IV Epiphanes, who declared himself God and tried to ban all other gods. The Nebuchadnezzar found in the other books of the Septuagint was King Nebuchadnezzar II of the Neo-Babylonian Empire between 605 and 562 BC. Nebuchadnezzar II was the son of Nabopolassar, an Assyrian official who rebelled against Assyria in 626 BC. Nebuchadnezzar II was the chief architect of the Neo-Babylonian Empire, who in 605 BC, after taking the throne, launched an invasion of Assyria and Syria with his Median allies, and defeated the Assyrians and Egyptians, and incorporated Syria and Phoenicia into his Empire.

If the text does date back to the Assyrian or Median Empires, then the original name of the king in the story must have been replaced with a more famous king at some point. A similar set of substitutions took place with the Book of Tobit, which is reflected between the two surviving copies, the common version found in the Codex Vaticanus and most other copies of the Septuagint, and the version in the Codex Sinaiticus, which is substantially different. The Sinaiticus version appears to be an older translation of Tobit, done in a different dialect than used at the Library of Alexandria, which someone decided to include in the Codex Sinaiticus instead of the Alexandrian translation. The Sinaiticus' version includes a historically valid version of the conquest of Nineveh by the Medes, while the Vaticanus version claims that the Babylonian King Nebuchadnezzar and the Persian King Xerxes (Ahasuerus / Ασυηρος) destroyed Nineveh, which is nonsense, as they lived a century apart, and neither destroyed Nineveh. Unfortunately, no known variant of Judith exists for comparison.

If this was originally a story written during the Assyrian or Median eras, the Assyrian king in question had to have been Ashurbanipal, who ruled Assyria between 668 and 627 BC. Several parallels are found between Ashurbanipal and the king in Judith, including the war against Elam, the general rebellion throughout his empire, and the conquest of Media, which resulted in the killing of the Median king. The only Assyrian king to do this was Ashurbanipal in year 17 of his reign, the same year listed in the book of Judith, who killed the Median king Phraortes (𒃰𒂖𒁺𒂖𒄩𒀞𒈪), which the book of Judith calls Arphaxad. In the same year, 653 BC, the Egyptians revolted with the aid of the Lydians, who broke their alliance with Assyria, and the following year Babylonia revolted with the backing of the Elamites. It is unclear how much of the Assyrian Empire revolted, however, Ashurbanipal spent years campaigning across his empire to restore it and never bothered trying to recapture Egypt, into which he had sent multiple armies to defend it from Kushite invasions earlier in his reign, before appointing Psamtik I as its pharaoh and slowly withdrawing his troops to suppress the rebellions across the empire.

2 Codex Vaticanus: Nineveh (ℵℹℵℰℽℋ)

Nineveh was a major city and occasionally the capital of the Assyrian Empire until 706 BC, when the capital was moved to Dur-Sharrukin. It was the capital of Ashurbanipal's empire, and was one of the largest cities in the world at the time, with between 100,000 and 150,000 inhabitants.

3 Codex Vaticanus: Arphaxad (ᴀᴘɸᴀᴤᴀᴅ)

There is no known Median king named Arphaxad. The Arphaxad (אַרְפַּכְשַׁד / Ἀρφαξάδ) found in the Torah was one of the sons of Shem, the son of Noah.

If the text does date back to the Assyrian or Media Empires, then the original name of the king in the story must have been replaced with a more famous name at some point. The only Median king who this story could have been about was Phraortes, who ruled Media between 675 and 653 BC. His Median name was Fravartish (𐎳𐎼𐎺𐎼𐎫𐎡𐏁), which was transliterated as Paarmartiiš (𒉺𒅈𒈥𒋾𒅖) in Elamite, Paarúmartiiš (𒉺𒌋𒈥𒋾𒅖) in Babylonian, Frauuaši (𐬫𐬀𐬀) in Avestan, Prwrt (פרורת) in Aramaic, and Phraortes (Φραόρτης) in Greek, from which the modern English name is derived. It is unclear how it would have been rendered in Aramaic, from which the Greek translation of Judith was presumably translated.

4 Codex Vaticanus: Mêdôn (ΜΗΔШΝ). Translation: Medes

The Medes built the Median empire in modern northern Iran and Iraq, and most of Turkey, before the rise of the Persian Empire.

5 Codex Vaticanus: Ecbatanoes (ΕΚΒΑΤΑΝΟΙC)

Ecbatana the Greek name of Hagmatana (𒃻𒌋𒐋𒐖𒁹𒈨𒀭𒈨𒌍𒅕), the capital of the Median Empire, and later the summer capital of the Persian Empire. Its name translates in Old Persian as 'the place of gathering.' The site of Ecbatana is generally regarded as having been Hamadān in western modern Iran, however, other sites have been suggested, including Takht-e Soleymān, and Tabriz, both in northwest modern Iran. Conversely, the book of Tobit suggests that Ecbatana was in the region of modern Tehran, in the plains near Ray, which the Book of Judith also implies in the following lines. It has also been suggested that there were several Hagmatanas in the Media empire, either moving seasonally, or between monarchs, however, this has yet to be proved conclusively.

6 Codex Vaticanus: Ragoes (ΡΑΓΟΙC)

Ray is an ancient city near Tehran in Iran. It is regarded as the oldest continuously inhabited city in Tehran Province, dating back to the Median Empire. Until around 300 years ago, it was the major city in the region, however, Tehran has grown rapidly in the past 300 years, and is 20 times the size of Ray today. The name Ray (ری) is derived from the Old

Persian Raga (𒌷𒂵𒉿), which the Greeks transliterated as Rágois (Ῥάγοις), Rhágai (Ῥάγαι), and Rháges (Ῥάγες), in various Greek dialects. It was transliterated into Latin as Rhagae and Rhaganae. The direct transliteration of the modern Persian name Ray is used in this translation, although it is also transliterated as Rey, Rayy, or Rhay.

7 Codex Vaticanus: Ydaspên (ⲨⲆⲀⲤⲦⲎⲚ), generally transliterated as Hydaspes in English

In Greek mythology, Hydaspes was the name of a river in India, which was the Greek name of a vast territory, including modern India, Pakistan, and Afghanistan. Hydaspes is believed to be the Jhelum River in northern modern Pakistan. The Hydaspes/Jhelum River was the site of a major battle between Alexander's armies and the Indian army of King Porus (Πῶρος), who was killed in battle. It is not clear who Porus was, as no records of someone with that name survive in Indian literature.

This river's name is inconsistent with the rest of the Assyrian-era story of Judith, and it was likely added during the Greek era to replace a Mesopotamian River that was less famous, or unknown to the Greeks and Judeans of the time. The use of the name Hydaspes in the text, and the fact that no known alternate version of Judith seems to have survived does make the book look like a Greek-era text, but it could easily date to an earlier era if the name Hydaspes replaced an older name, like the substitutions that took place in the books of Tobit. If the name of Mesopotamian river was replaced, it was most likely the name Harpasos ('Αρπασος), which is believed to have been the early Greek name for the Karasu River in modern Turkey or the Çoruh River in modern Turkey and Georgia. Sometime after the conquest of Alexander, the Karasu was renamed Têleboas (Τηλεβόας), and the Çoruh was renamed the Acampsis (Ἀκαμψις).

However, in Xenophon's Anabasis, written between 401 and 354 BC, he referred to a river in the region as the Harpasos. In Anabasis, Xenophon recounted the march of the Greek mercenary forces into Persian-held Anatolia in 401 BC, hired by the Persian prince Cyrus the Younger, who was attempting to usurp the throne from his brother Artaxerxes II. It is not clear which river he was referencing, however, based on the path the Greeks took through Anatolia, scholars believe it was either the Karasu or the Çoruh. The Karasu is a long river in eastern modern Turkey that flows into the Euphrates, and was within the Assyrian Empire, while the Çoruh is a fast-flowing river in modern northeast Turkey and Georgia, which flows into the Black Sea and was not under the control of the Assyrian Empire, therefore, the reference would have likely been to the Karasu.

The name Harpasos itself, regardless of which river it applied to, was a Greek transliteration of the local name of the river, which had been lost by the time the Library of Alexandria translated Judith, however, if Judith was originally written during the Assyrian, Median, or Persian eras, the text would have been written in Aramaic, Neo-Assyrian, Neo-Babylnian, Mede, or Old Persian, all of which would have used the original name of the river, not the later Greek name. This means that the Greeks would not have known which river the name applied to in their language, and seem to have substituted a famous and similarly named Greek river. While this substitution of Harpasos with Hydaspes is entirely theoretical, it certainly makes more sense than the inclusion of Indian armies with the Mesopotamian armies in the era before the rise of the Persian Empire. This, however, does require the text to date back to the Assyrian, Mede, or Persian eras, which therefore also requires a number of substitutions to have taken place throughout the text.

8 Codex Vaticanus: Arioch (ΑΡΙѠΧ)

The plains of Arioch are a reference to the plains of Iraq, which was also known as the land of Uruk since the time of Sumer.

9 Codex Vaticanus: Elymaeôn (ΕΛΥΜΑΙѠΝ)

Elam was an ancient nation in southern modern Iran, known as Haltamti (𒄷𒁴𒋾) in Elamite. Its modern name is derived from its Sumerian name Elam^{ki} (𒉏𒆠), via the Neo-Babylonian name Elamma^{ki} (𒉏𒈠𒆠), and Hebrew Eilam (עֵילָם). The Greek name Elymaes (Ἐλυμαῖσ) appears to have been independently derived from the Babylonian name. The Greek term used here, referred to the people from Elam, commonly called Elamites today.

During the era of Ashurbanipal, who appears to have been the original Assyrian king in the story, Elam attacked Assyria, in 655 BC, when they launched an invasion of Babylonia. King Ashurbanipal marched his army south to liberate Babylonia, and then into Elam, where the Assyrian armies defeated the Elamite armies. The Elamite king Teumman was beheaded, and the capital city of Susa was razed to the ground, however, the Assyrians could not consolidate their victory and integrate Elam into the empire, because of a revolt in the Assyrian Empire, which caused Ashurbanipal to withdraw his troops from Elam, exactly like the king in the book of Judith.

After the Assyrian army withdrew, the Elamites attempted to rebuild, and backed the revolutionaries within the Assyrian Empire, however, after dealing with the rebellions, Ashurbanipal's armies returned to Elam, and completely destroyed it in 639 BC. Elam was nominally integrated into the empire, however, was occupied by Persians, who over the following decades absorbed the remnants of the Elamites into their culture.

10 Codex Vaticanus: Cheleoud (Ⲭⲉⲗⲉⲟⲩⲇ)

The Chaldeans were the ancient Semitic people that conquered the Old Babylonian empire before the time of Abraham, and became another name for Babylonians in later periods.

11 Codex Vaticanus: Esdrêlôn (ЄⲤⲆⲢⲎⲖⲰⲚ).

Esdrêlôn (Εσδρηλων) was the Greek transliteration of Yizre'el (יזרעאל), the valley in northern modern Israel, which has also been transliterated as Jezreel.

12 Codex Vaticanus: Batanê (ⲂⲀⲦⲀⲚⲎ)

Given the name is listed among other places in the region of ancient Judah, it is likely this is Bethany (Βηθανία), however, the name is transliterated differently than it was in the Gospels. The location of Bethany is not known for sure, however, within the Islamic world, is accepted as the Palestinian town of al-Azariya (العيزرية) in the West Bank, which is named after Lazarus, who lived in Bethany in the Gospel of John. The town was renamed after Lazarus by Christians in the 4th century, and it is unclear if it was ever known as Bethany before the 1800s, when Catholic and Protestant Christians dubbed it 'Bethany.'

Given its proximity to Jerusalem, and the fact that it would have been in Judah at the time, this cannot have been the city the text is referring to. The Aramaic name of Bethany is byt ônya (ביתא עניא), which means 'house of suffering,' which appears to be where this alternate Greek transliteration originates, and supports the existence of an Aramaic version of Judith. Conversely, the normal Greek transliteration of Bethany (Βηθανία), is believed to be a transliteration of the Hebrew byt ôny (בית עני), meaning 'house of poor,' however, this is also debated, as it does not appear in any known text earlier than the Gospels.

13 Codex Vaticanus: Taphnas (ΤΑΦΝΑϹ)

The city of Tahpanhes was located in Egypt, on the shore of Lake Manzala, along the Tanitic branch of the Nile. The more common English name is derived from the Hebrew name Tachpanches (תְּחְפַּנְחֵס). The Greeks renamed the city Daphnae hae Pêlousiae (Δάφναι αἱ Πηλούσιαι), however, the name Taphnas (Ταφνας) was used in the Septuagint's books of Jeremiah and Ezekiel, suggesting these books were translated before the name of the city was changed, likely during the reign of King Ptolemy II Philadelphus and his sister-wife Queen Arsineo II, before the Nile-Red Sea Canal was opened in circa 270 BC. Philadelphus and Arsineo were both fascinated with ancient Egyptian culture, and Philadelphus was considered to be the founder of the Library of Alexandria, although some ancient records claim it was his father Ptolemy I Soter.

In addition to the Egyptian records, Philadelphus apparently studied the Greek translations of the Aramaic texts that involved Egypt, and used the Aramaic names found in the ancient Samaritan and Judean texts to name the cities he rebuilt along the Nile-Red Sea Canal. The more common Hebrew-derived Tahpanhes is used in this translation, however, the name found in the Septuagint is likely a direct transliteration of the older Aramaic version of the name.

14 Codex Vaticanus: Ramessê (ⲣⲁⲙⲉⲥⲥⲏ)

This city had multiple names over the millennia, including Avaris, Pi-Ramesses, and finally Ramesses. Avaris was the capital of the Hyksos in Egypt, which was virtually destroyed as the Thebeans drove the Hyksos from Egypt. The city was rebuilt on the outskirts of the ruins of Avaris as Pi-Ramesses during the Ramesside Period of the later New Kingdom. It was abandoned for a century after the river silted up in 1060 BC, however, rebuilt as Ramesses around 125 years later by Shoshenq I who was trying to restore the prestige of Egypt.

15 Codex Vaticanus: Aethiopias (ⲁⲓⲑⲓⲟⲡⲓⲁⲥ).

Aethiopia was the Greek name of sub-Saharan Africa. The equivalent in the Masoretic texts in other books was Kûš (כּוּשׁ), the ancient empire in Sudan.

16 The seventeenth year of this king, is clearly a reference to the seventeenth year of King Ashurbanipal, who faced a rebellion in his 17th year, 653 BC, by the various peoples mentioned in the preceding verses. This happened while he was campaigning in Media, where he killed King Phraortes. After the revolt of 653 BC, most of the empire was reconsolidated by Ashurbanipal, however, Egypt was not reoccupied. In the Median power vacuum, the Scythians occupied Media for twenty-eight years until Phraortes's son Cyaxares led a revolt, and reunited the Medes, following which he formed an alliance with the Babylonians to conquered the Assyrians, and also then conquered the Lydians, forming an Empire the stretched from the Aegean Sea to the Caspian Sea.

Judith: Chapter 2

In the eighteenth year, the twenty-second day of the first month, there was talk in the palace of King Nebuchadnezzar of the Assyrians that he should, as he had said, avenge himself on all the earth. So he called all his officers and nobles to him and covertly made plans to conquer the whole earth. They decreed to destroy all flesh that did not obey the commandments of his mouth.

When he had ended his counsel, Nebuchadnezzar, king of the Assyrians called Holofernes the chief captain of his army, who was second only to him, and said, "This, says the great king, the lord of the whole earth, 'Look, you will go out from my presence, and take your men that are confident in their own strength, a hundred and twenty thousand infantry, and twelve thousand cavalry. You will go against all the western countries because they disobeyed my commandment. Tell them to prepare the earth and the water, for I am coming in my fury against them and the feet of my armies will cover the whole face of the earth, and my troops will plunder them. Their slain will fill their valleys and brooks, and the rivers will be filled with their dead until they overflow. I will take captives to the furthest parts of all the earth. You will go beforehand for me and capture all their lands, and if they will surrender themselves to you, you will keep them for me until the day of their punishment. But those that resist, don't spare them, slaughter them and plunder from them wherever you go. For as I live, and by the power of my kingdom, whatever I have spoken I will do by my hand. Make sure that you don't break any of the commandments of your lord, but accomplish them fully as I have commanded you."

Then Holofernes went out from the presence of his lord and called all the governors and captains, and the officers of the Assyrian army. He mustered the chosen men for the battle as his lord had commanded him, a hundred and twenty thousand infantry, and twelve thousand archers on horseback. He organized them into a great army and marshaled them for the war. He took camels and donkeys for their chariots in great numbers, and sheep and oxen and goats without counting for their provision, plenty of food for every man of the army, and a great deal of gold and silver out of the king's palace. Then he set out with his army to go in advance of King Nebuchadnezzar in the expedition, and to cover the face of the earth to the west with their chariots, and cavalry, and their elite infantry. A great number also from the sundry countries traveled with them like locusts, and like the sand of the earth, for the multitude was without number.

They went out of Nineveh three days' journey towards the plain of Bektileth[1] and camped near

Bektileth in the mountains that are near upper Cilicia.[2] Then he took all his army, his infantry, cavalry, and chariots, and went from there into the hill country, and destroyed Phoud[3] and Lydia,[4] and he captured all the children of Rassis,[5] and the Ishmaelites[6] who were near the wilderness to the south of the land around the capital.[7] Then he crossed over the Euphrates and traveled through Mesopotamia, and destroyed all the high cities that were on the river, and crossed[8] when he was near the sea. He conquered the lands of Cilicia, and slaughtered all that resisted him, and came to the borders of Japheth, which were to the south near Arabia. He surrounded all the Midianites[9] and burnt their tents, and destroyed their sheepfolds.

Then he went down into the plain of Damascus in the time of wheat harvest, and burnt up all their fields, and destroyed their flocks and herds, also he attacked their cities, and completely devastated their countries, and slaughtered all their young men with the edge of the sword. The fear and dread of him fell on all the inhabitants of the sea lands which were in Sidon, Tyre and those that lived in Sur,[10] and Okina,[11] and all that lived in Yavne,[12] and those that lived in Ashdod,[13] and Ashkelon[14] were terrified of him.

Judith: Chapter 2 Notes

1 Codex Vaticanus: Bectileth (ΒΕΚΤΙΛΕΘ)

The Greek term does not appear to be a proper name of a place in the region, however, based on the described geography, the location would have been in the region of the Cilician Gates (Gülek Pass), which is a pass through the Taurus Mountains connecting the lowlands of Cilicia to the Anatolian Plateau. The Cilician Gates have been fortified since at least 4500 BC, and the ruins of several fortified towns exist in the region. Bectileth may be the name of a fortified town in the region, however, if it was, it is not clear when the settlement existed.

2 Codex Vaticanus: Cilicias (ΚΙΛΙΚΙΑC)

Cilicia is the ancient name of the southeastern coast of Turkey.

3 Codex Vaticanus: Phoud (ΦΟΥΔ)

As the land was described as being between Cilicia and Lydia, it would likely mean the original reference to Phrygia, which was on the road from Lydia to Cilicia. It is not clear why the name Phoud would have been in the texts, as that was the name of the Libyans of the Western Desert Oases and Cyrene. It is possible that a translator did not recognize the original name and substituted a more common term from his time.

Ashurbanipal's armies are the only Assyrian forces ever recorded as having traveled along this road, in 665 BC en route to Lydia, which supports this text have originated about him.

4 Codex Vaticanus: Loud (ⲗⲟⲩⲇ)

Loud was the ancient Hebrew name for Lydia, the ancient civilization in Southwest Turkey. Like the previous reference to Phoud, this appears to be a reference to the early campaigns of King Ashurbanipal, who sent a major force into Lydia to repulse a Cimmerian invasion in 665 BC. The Cimmerians, who lived in ancient Ukraine and southern Russia, tried to invade Assyria in the era of Ashurbanipal's father, King Esarhaddon, and were defeated by the Assyrians. When Lydia, in western Anatolia, was invaded, the king of Lydia, King Gyges, sent to Assyria for assistance, and the two countries, which had formerly not had a formal relationship became allies. The army of Ashurbanipal did drive the Cimmerians out of Lydia, however, appear to have also plundered Lydia, and the alliance between the two countries was tenuous at best.

The alliance lasted until 653 BC, when the Assyrians conquered the Medes, and Lydia broke the alliance with Assyria by sending troops to Egypt to back King Psamtik I's successful revolt. Ashurbanipal was the only Assyrian king who is recorded as sending troops to Lydia, so if this story was originally written in the Assyrian or Median Empires, he is the king called 'Nebuchadnezzar' in the text. The Lydians did request assistance of the Assyrians again after the Cimmerians returned in 652 BC, however, there is no evidence of the

Assyrians sent support, and King Gyges was killed fighting the Cimmerians.

5 Codex Vaticanus: Rassis (ρ∧ccιc)

• Codes Alexandrinus: Rassis (ρ∧ccειc)

The codices contain alternate transliterations of the same name, indicating that the Greek translators did not know its Greek translation. Several possible translations have been proposed, including that it is the name of an individual, Arab tribe, or foreign nation. Variations of the name Rassis are sometimes mentioned in Neo-Assyrian records along side the Scythians, suggesting they were mercenaries. If it started as an ethnic term, it may have began as a reference to the Etruscans of northern Italy. The Etruscans called themselves the Rassena (ᴅɴɴᴇsᴅᴩ), while the name 'Etruscan' was ultimately derived from the early Greek name for them: Tyrsênoe (Τυρσηνοι), essentially meaning 'tower people,' as their cities were built on hills.

This term appears to have been unknown even when the Septuagint was translated, and therefore is transliterated directly in this translation, using the older Codex Vaticanus spelling.

6 Codex Vaticanus: Ishmail (ιcᴍ∧н∧)

Ishmaelites is a term that refers to several Arabian tribes in the ancient Israelites books who are said to be the descendants of Abraham via his son Ishmael. The Nabateans appear to be one of these groups. The Nabateans lived in northwest Arabia, and it is generally believed that their later capital was Petra in Jordan. King Ashurbanipal is recorded as defeating a people called the Nabaiti, who are generally assumed to be the Nabateans, although most records of them date to a later period.

7 Codex Vaticanus: Cheleon (ⲭⲉⲗⲉⲱⲛ)

This word is a direct transliteration of kôlywn (כעליון), which would translate as 'the capital' or 'of the chief.' The Greek name in the text is unknown from the historical record, and so the word is assumed to be a transliteration error at the Library of Alexandria, and the Semitic term is translated instead. This word does prove the existence of a Semitic source text for the Book of Judith, however, it is not clear whether the text was Aramaic or Hebrew from this one word. It is also possible that one of the Ishmaelite tribes had a settlement called 'capital,' but it is more likely that this a reference to Dumat al-Jandal, the ancient capital of the Dumah Tribe of Ishmaelites. The name translates as 'Dumat of the Stones,' while the Akkadian (Assyrian) name was Adummatu. Today the ruins of the city lay in northern Saudi Arabia.

During the time of Ashurbanipal, the Qedarites attacked the Amorites within the Assyrian Empire, and were defeated, following which Ashurbanipal boasted that he put a chain around their King Ammuladi's neck and made him guard the dog kennels.

8 Codex Vaticanus: Abrôna (ΑΒΡѠΝΑ)

The word does not appear to be a proper name, but a transliteration of the Assyrian word ebēru (𒂊), which translates as 'to cross.' This suggests the Book of Judith was written of translated into cuneiform, which was the official script of the Neo-Assyrian Empire, and used alongside Aramaic in the Neo-Babylonian Empire. If so, it must have been written before the Neo-Babylonian Empire fell to the Persians, in 539 BC.

Based on the described movements of the army, this appears to be the only rational translation of the texts, as they started in the Arabian Desert, following which they crossed the Euphrates, and then 'Abrona' following which they were back at the Mediterranean Sea at Cilicia. Therefore the Akkadian term is restored in this translation.

9 Codex Vaticanus: Madiam (ΜΑΔΙΑΜ)

The Greek name Midiam is more commonly transliterated as Midian in English, based on the Hebrew version of the name Midyan (מִדְיָן). The mountains of Midian (مَدْيَن) are located in northwestern Saudi Arabia along the Gulf of Aqaba.

10 Codex Vaticanus: Shur (ⲥ**ⲟ**ⲩⲣ)

Sur was, and still is, the local name for Tyre (صور), which is already mentioned in the text. The English name Tyre is derived from the Greek name Týros (Τύρος), which was in use by the Greeks since at least the 5th century BC. The local Canaanite name was Ṣr (𐤑𐤓), which meant 'rocks,' as there was a rocky harbor there, with a rocky island off the shore. At the time the story is set, the island and coastal town were two settlements under a common government, both called Sur.

The island had originally tried to remain independent when the Assyrians conquered the coastal city, relying on Tyre's distant colonies in North Africa to sustain it, however, once the Assyrians built a Mediterranean fleet, the island had surrendered to Assyria. The inclusion of the second reference to Tyre/Ṣr is therefore valid in the era, and seems to be absolute proof that the original Book of Judith predates Alexander the Great constructing a causeway out the island in order to conquer it. Since Alexander's time, the two settlements have been one town, and there would have been no reason to mention them separately.

11 Codex Vaticanus: Okina (ⲟⲕⲓⲛⲁ)

This is generally accepted as a reference to Acre, on modern Israel's northern Mediterranean coast. The spelling of the name is odd because the Greeks generally spelled it as Acra (Ἄκρα) or Acê (Ἀκη), which is similar to the Neo-Babylonian cuneiform Ak^ki (𒀝𒆠), Phoenician Ôk (𐤀𐤊), Egyptian Ôkå (𓂝𓎡), and Hebrew Akkô (עַכּוֹ). The location of Okina, along the coast between Tyre and Yavne indicates it was a reference to Acre. The spelling of the name suggests that it was a transliteration error during a translation from Canaanite to Aramaic, where a Canaanite R (𐤓) was replaced with an Aramaic N (𐡍). This suggests the book started in Judahite or Samaritan before being translated into Aramaic.

12 Codex Vaticanus: Iemnaan (ιϵΜΝΑΑΝ)

The City of Yavne (יַבְנֶה) was called Iemnaan (Ιεμνααν) or Jamnia (Ἰαμνία) by the ancient Greeks. Yavne is a coastal city in Israel, south of modern Tel Aviv-Yafo.

13 Codex Vaticanus: Azôtô (ΑΖΩΤΩ)

This is the Greek name of Ashdod (אַשְׁדּוֹד), a port city on the modern Israeli southern Mediterranean coast, north of Ashkelon.

14 Codex Vaticanus: Ascalôni (ΑϹΚΑΛΩΝΙ)

This is the Greek name of Ashkelon (אַשְׁקְלוֹן). Ashkelon is a port city on the modern Israeli southern Mediterranean coast, south of Ashkelon, and north of the Palestinian Gaza Strip.

Judith: Chapter 3

They sent ambassadors to him to request peace, saying, "Look, we the servants of Nebuchadnezzar the great king lie in front of you, use us as will be good in your sight. Look, our houses, and all our places, and all our fields of wheat, and flocks, and herds, and all the lodges of our tents lie in front of you, use them as it pleases you. Look, even our cities and the inhabitants of are your servants, come and deal with them as seems good to you."

So the men came to Holofernes and told him this. Then he came down towards the sea coast, along with his army, and set garrisons in the high cities, and took from them elite men for aid. They and all the country around received them with garlands, with dances, and with timbrels. Yet he tore down their frontiers and cut down their groves,[1] for he had decreed to destroy all the gods of the land, that all nations should worship only Nebuchadnezzar, and that all tongues and tribes should praise him as God. Also, he came up against Yizre'el near Judah, just across the great ridge of Judah. He camped between Gibeon[2] and Scythopolis,[3] and there he waited a whole month, so he could assemble all the chariots of his army.

Judith: Chapter 3 Notes

1 Codex Vaticanus: alsê (ⲀⲀⲤⲎ). Translation: grove (or woods

• Leningrad Codex (in other books): Asherah (אֲשֵׁרָה). Translation: sacred grove

Asherah was the name of an Israelite goddess before the time of Elijah in the 9th century, described as the mother of Yahweh, as well as the wife of El or Ba'al. She appears to have been worshiped by planting oak trees, like here Middle Kingdom era Egyptian equivalent Iusaaset, who was worshiped by planting acacia trees. Like Asherah, Atum's wife Iusaaset was merged with Hathor during the New Kingdom Era. This reference to the Asherahs being cut down is almost certainly a reference to the oak trees that the ancient Canaanites used to mark important graves.

2 Codex Vaticanus: Gaibai (ⲄⲀⲒⲂⲀⲒ)

Gibeon is an ancient city directly north of Jerusalem.

3 Codex Vaticanus: Scythôn (ⲤⲔⲨⲐⲰⲚ)

Scythôn, later called Scythopolis, is the ancient Greek name of Beit She'an, a city in northern Israel. It was named Scythopolis by the Greeks because Scythians settled in the area during the Persian administration of the region.

Judith: Chapter 4

Now the Israelites that lived in Judah, heard all that Holofernes, the chief captain of King Nebuchadnezzar of Assyria, had done to the nations, and in what manner he had plundered all their temples, and reduced them to nothing. Therefore, they were very afraid of him and were concerned for Jerusalem, and for the Temple of Lord God.[1] They were newly returned from the captivity, and all the people of Judah were lately gathered together, and the vessels, and the altar, and the temple were sanctified after the profanation. Therefore, they sent messages to all the lands of Samaria, and the villages, and to Bethoron, Belmen, Jericho, Hobah, Esora, and to the valley of Salem. They occupied all the hilltops and fortified the villages that were on them, and stored up food for the provision of war, for their fields were recently reaped.

Also, Jehoiakim the high priest, who was in those days in Jerusalem, wrote to those who lived in Baetyloua, and Betomestham, which is near Yizre'el towards the open country, near to Dothan, ordering them to hold the roads through the hill country, for through them was the entrance into Judah, and it was easy to stop anyone that would come through because the passage was only wide enough for two men at the most.

The Israelites did as Jehoiakim the high priest and the elders of all the people of Israel who lived in Jerusalem had commanded them. Then every man of Israel cried to God with great fervency, and with great vehemency, they humiliate their souls. They, and their wives and their children, and their livestock, and every foreigner and employee, and their slaves bought with money, put sackcloth on their loins. Every man and woman, and the little children, and the inhabitants of Jerusalem, fell before the temple, and threw ashes on their heads, and spread out their sackcloth before the face of the Lord. Also, they put sackcloth around the altar, and cried to the god in Israel, that he would not give their children to be slaughtered, and their wives as plunder, and the cities of their inheritance to destruction, and the sanctuary to profanation and reproach, and for the nations to rejoice at.

God heard their prayers, and looked on their concerns, for the people fasted many days in all Judah and Jerusalem before the sanctuary of the holy Lord Omnipotent.[2] Jehoiakim the high priest, and all the priests that stood before the Lord, and those who served the Lord had their loins girded with sackcloth, and offered the daily burnt offerings, with the vows and free gifts of the people, and had ashes on their miters, and cried to the Lord with all their power, that he would look on all the houses of Israel graciously.

Judith: Chapter 4 Notes

1 Codex Vaticanus: cyriou theou (ΚΥΡΙΟΥΘΕΟΥ). Translation: Lord God

2 Codex Vaticanus: cyriou pantocratoros (ΚΥΡΙΟΥ ΠΑΝΤΟΚΡΑΤΟΡΟΣ). Translation: Lord Omnipotent (or Almighty)

The Septuagint's 'omnipotent' (παντοκράτορος) is generally mirrored by the term Shaddai (שַׁדַּי) in the Masoretic Text, including 33 times in the books of Job. In Bereshít, the Masoretic version of Cosmic Genesis, the god of Abraham, Isaac, and Jacob is known as Shaddai, however, the Greek translation does not include 'omnipotent' or any alternative term, suggesting it was never translated into the Aramaic version of Genesis. The genealogy of nations found in Cosmic Genesis Chapter 10, includes Aramaic terms, and dates itself to have been written between 715 and 706 BC, indicating that the removal of the name Shaddai in the Aramaic version of Genesis was probably part of King Hezekiah's anti-Mosaic reforms between 715 and 687 BC.

According to 4th Kingdoms (Masoretic Kings), Hezekiah's reforms were reversed by his son Manasseh, who ruled Judah between 687-643 BC, and therefore was the king in 653 BC, when the original story was probably set. As the Greek translation was almost certainly a translation of Shaddai, the name is restored in the restoration.

Judith: Chapter 5

When Holofernes, the chief captain of the armies of Assyria, heard that the Israelites had prepared for war, and had blocked the roads through the hill country, and had fortified all the hilltops and had laid impediments to his campaign in those countries, he was very angry and called all the princes of Moab, and the captains of Amman, and all the governors of the sea coast. He said to them, "Tell me now, you sons of Canaan, who are these people that dwell in the hill country? What are the cities that they inhabit, and how large are their armies? What is their power and strength, and what king rules over them, or captain of their army? Why have they determined not to come and meet me, like the inhabitants of the west?"

Then Achior, the captain of all the Ammanites said, "Let my lord now hear a word from the mouth of your servant, and I will declare to you the truth concerning these people, who dwell near you, and inhabits the hill countries, and no lie will come out of the mouth of your servant. These people are descended from the Chaldeans. They previously lived in Mesopotamia, but because they would not follow the gods of their fathers, who were in the land of Chaldea, they left the way of their ancestors and worshiped the god Shamayim,[1] the god who they knew. They drove them out from before their gods, and they fled into Mesopotamia, and stayed there many days."

"Then their god commanded them to leave from the place where they stayed and to go into the land of Canaan, where they lived and were increased with gold and silver, and with very much livestock. But when a famine covered all the land of Canaan, they went down into Egypt, and stayed there, while they were nourished, and became there a great multitude, so that one could not number their nation. Therefore, the king of Egypt rose up against them, and dealt cleverly with them, and brought them low with laboring in brick-making and made them slaves. Then they cried to their god, and he struck all the land of Egypt with incurable plagues, so the Egyptians cast them out of their sight. God dried the Papyrus Sea[2] before them, led them along the road to Sinai, and Kadesh-Barne, and drove out all that lived in the wilderness, so they lived in the land of the Amorites, and they slaughtered all of the people of Heshbon, and passed across the Jordan they possessed all the hill country."

"They drove out before them the Canaanites, Perizzites, Jebusites, Shechem,[3] and all the Girgashites, and they lived in that country many days. While they did not sin before their god, they prospered, because the god that hates iniquity was with them. But when they departed from the way which he appointed them, they were destroyed in many terrible battles and were led captives into a land that was not theirs, and the Temple of God was torn to the ground, and their cities were taken by the enemies."

"Now they have returned to their god, and have come back from the places where they were scattered, and have possessed Jerusalem, where their sanctuary is, and are seated in the hill country, yet before it was desolate. Now, therefore, my lord and governor, if there is any error against these people, and they sin against their god, let us consider that this will be their ruin, and let us go up, and we will conquer them. But if there is no iniquity in their nation, let my lord now pass by, in case their god defends them, and we become a reproach before all the world."

When Achior finished sayings this, all the people standing around the tent murmured, and the chief men of Holofernes and all that lived by the seaside and in Moab said that he should kill him. For they said, "We will not be afraid of the Israelites! Look it is a people that have no strength or will for a strong battle. Now, therefore, Lord Holofernes, we will go up, and they will be prey to be devoured by all your army."

Judith: Chapter 5 Notes

1 Codex Vaticanus: theô tou ouranou (ϴЄШΤΟΥ ΟΥΡΑΝΟΥ). Translation: god the Uranus (or vaulted-sky)

The Hebrew translation of Uranus (Οὐρανοῦ) was Shamayim (שָׁמַיִם) the god of the vaulted-skies. Shamayim was an early-Israelite god which appears to have been another name for the Canaanite god Baitlyos (𐤋𐤀 𐤕𐤉𐤏).

2 Codex Vaticanus: erythran thalassan (ЄΡΥϴΡΑΝ ϴΑΛΑϹϹΑΝ). Translation: Erythrean Sea

The Greek term is not geographically specific, allowing for the Israelites to have passed from Egypt to the wilderness at any point in the Red Sea or even the Gulf of Aden. The Greek name appears to be a translation of the Persian term Erostras, which referred to the entire Persian Gulf, Red Sea, and the Indian Ocean. The Greeks were likely referring to the Gulf of Suez, however, this was known to the ancient Egyptians as the 'Sea of Calm,' which is what the Israelites would have called it if that was where they were. The Hebrew term used in the Masoretic Text, in other books, was yam-sûp (יַם־סוּף), meaning 'Sea of papyrus.' This was not geographically specific either, however, does match the description of the shallow Lake Bardawil which has been a major source for papyrus reeds throughout Egyptian history, and is along the described route in Exodus. The name was transliterated directly once in the Codex Vaticanus' book of Judges, as thalassês Siph (θαλάσσης Σιφ), meaning Sea of Siph, and therefore the Hebrew and Aramaic name is restored in this translation.

3 Codex Vaticanus: Sychem (ϲϒⲭⲉⲙ)

In the ancient Israelite books of the Kingdoms, Shechem was the ancient capital of Israel before Jerusalem was captured.

Judith: Chapter 6

When the argument among men that were around the council ended, Holofernes the chief captain of the Assyrian army said to Achior, and before the Moabites and all the company of other nations, "Who are you, Achior? The mercenary of Ephraim?[1] You have prophesied against us as today, and have said that we should not make war with the people of Israel because their god will defend them? Who is a god other than Nebuchadnezzar? He will send his power and will destroy them from the face of the earth, and their god will not deliver them. We, his servants will destroy them to the last man, for they are not able to stop the power of our horses. With them we will tread them underfoot, and their mountains will be drunk with their blood, and their fields will be filled with their dead bodies, and their infantry will not be able to stand before us, for they will completely perish. So says King Nebuchadnezzar, lord of all the earth."

He said, "None of my words will be in vain. You, Achior, an employee of Amman, who have spoken these words in the day of your iniquity, will see my face no more from this day until I take vengeance of this nation that came out of Egypt. Then the sword of my army and the multitude of those who serve me will slaughter you, and you will fall among their dead when I return. Now my servants will take you back into the hill country, and will send you to one of the cities of the passages. You will not perish until you are destroyed with them. If you convince yourself in your mind that they will be taken, don't be depressed, as I have spoken it, and none of my words will be in vain."

Then Holofernes commanded his servants that waited in his tent, to take Achior, and bring him to Beitillu,[2] and deliver him into the hands of the Israelites. So his servants took him and brought him out of the camp into the plain, and they went from the middle of the plain into the hill country and came to the fountains that were under Beitillu. When the men of the city saw them, they picked up their weapons and went out of the city to the hilltops, and every man that used a sling kept them from coming up by slinging of stones against them. Nevertheless having sneaked to the foot of the hill, they tied up Achior, and threw him down, and left him at the foot of the hill, and returned to their lord.

The Israelites descended from their city, and came to him, and untied him, and brought him to Beitillu, and presented him to the governors of the city, which were in those days Uzziah the son of Micha, of the tribe of Simeon, and Chabris the son of Othniel, and Charmis the son of Malchiel. They called together all the elders of the city, and all their youths ran together, and their women, to the assembly, and they set Achior among their people. Then Uzziah asked him what was done. He answered and declared to them the words of the council of Holofernes, and all the words that he had spoken among the Assyrian princes, and what Holofernes had said proudly against the house of Israel.

Then the people fell and worshiped God, and cried to God, saying, "Lord God Shamayim, look at their pride, and pity the low estate of our nation, and look on the face of those that are sanctified to you this day."

Then they comforted Achior and praised him greatly. Uzziah took him out of the assembly to his house and made a feast to the elders, and they called on the god of Israel all that night for help.

Judith: Chapter 6 Notes

1 Codex Vaticanus: Ephraem (ЄⲪⲢⲀⲒⲘ). Translation: Ephraim

The Tribe of Ephraim was one of the tribes in the Kingdom of Samaria before the Assyrians conquered them in 723 BC. Several major cities of the kingdom were in the tribe's territory, including Bethel and Shiloh. The first monarch of Samaria was an Ephraimite named Jeroboam, and the tribe appears to have dominated the country of Samaria to the point that Ephraim was used as a synonym for Israel before Assyria's conquest of Samaria.

2 Codex Vaticanus: Baetyloua (ⲂⲀⲒⲦⲨⲀⲞⲨⲀ)

This is not a city whose name is otherwise documented in ancient literature, however, it is likely the town of Beitillu (بيت إللو), in the modern Palestinian West Bank, northwest of Jerusalem. Beitillu appears to have been inhabited continuously from the era of the old kingdoms, and would have been at the border of Judah and Assyria at the time. The name of the town has not changed significantly over the centuries and was recorded as Bayt Illu in the Ottoman tax register of 1596.

Judith: Chapter 7

The next day, Holofernes commanded all his army, and his people who had come serve him, that they should move their camp towards Beitillu, to capture the roads into the hill country, and to make war against the Israelites. They moved their camps that day, and the army was 170,000 infantry, and 12,000 cavalry, beside the baggage, and other men that were on foot among them in very great numbers. They camped in the valley near Beitillu, by the fountain, and they covered a wide area around Dothan[1] to Belbaem[2] and on to Cyamonos,[3] which is near Yizre'el.

Now when the Israelites saw the multitude of them, they were greatly troubled, and said to each other, "These men will consume the face of the earth. The high mountains, and the valleys, and the hills are unable to carry their weight."

Then every man took up his weapons of war, and when they had started fires in their towers, they remained and watched all that night. But on the second day, Holofernes brought out all his cavalry in the sight of the Israelites which were in Beitillu, and viewed the passages up to the city, and went to the fountains of their waters, and took them, and set garrisons of soldiers at them, and he left to return to his people.

Then all the chiefs of the children of Esau and all the governors of the Moabites, and the captains of the sea coast came to him and said, "Let our lord now hear our word, that your army is not defeated, as these people of Israel do not trust in their spears, but in the height of the mountains in which they live, because it is not easy to come up to the tops of their mountains. Now, therefore, my lord, don't fight against them in battle formation, and not even one of your men will die. Remain in your camp, and keep all the men of your army, and let your servants take into their hands the fountain of water, which issues out of the foot of the mountain."

"All the inhabitants of Beitillu get their water there, so thirst will kill them, and they will give up their city. We and our people will go up to the nearby hilltops and will camp on them, to watch that none leave the city, so they and their wives and their children will be consumed with fire, and before the sword that comes against them, they will be slaughtered in the streets where they live. Thereby will you award them for their evil in rebelling, and not meeting you peaceably."

These words pleased Holofernes and all his servants, and he appointed them to do as they had suggested. So the camp of the Ammanites departed, and with them, five thousand of the Assyrians, and they camped in the valley and captured the waters and the fountains of the waters of the Israelites. Then the children of Esau went up with the children of Amman and camped in the hill country near Dothan, and they sent some of them towards the south, and towards the east near Aqraba,[4] which is near to Chous,[5] that is on the River Mishmar[6], and the rest of the army of the Assyrians camped in the plain and covered the surface of the whole land. Their tents and chariots were camped in great numbers.

Then the Israelites cried out to the Lord God because they were afraid of all the enemies that had surrounded them, and there was no way to escape them. For thirty-four days the armies of Assyria remained camped around them with their infantry, chariots, and cavalry so that all the water store ran low for the inhabitants of Beitillu. The cisterns were empty and they had not drunk their fill of water, as they were rationing it. Their young children were scared, and their women and young men fainted for thirst and fell down in the streets of the city, and by the passages of the gates, and there was no longer any strength in them.

Then all the people assembled to Uzziah, and to the chief of the city, both young men, and women, and children, and cried with a loud voice, and said before all the elders, "God judge between us and you, for you have done us great injury in that you have not sought peace with the Assyrians. For now, we have no helper, but

God has sold us into their hands, that we should be thrown down before them with thirst and great destruction. Now, therefore, call them to you, and deliver the whole city for plunder to the people of Holofernes, and to all his army. For it is better for us to be plundered by them than to die of thirst! We will be his slaves so that our souls may live and not see the death of our infants before our eyes, or our wives, or our children. We take as a witness against you Shamayim and Eretz,[7] and our god,[8] and Lord of our fathers,[9] who punishes us according to our sins and the sins of our fathers, that he does not, as we have said this day."

There was great weeping with one consent in the middle of the assembly, and they cried to the Lord God with a loud voice. Then Uzziah replied to them, "Brothers, be of good courage, let us endure five more days, during which time the Lord God may turn his mercy towards us, for he will not forsake us completely. If these days pass, and there comes no help for us, I will do according to your words."

He dispersed the people, everyone to their own posts, and they went to the walls and towers of their city and sent the women and children into their houses, and they were very depressed in the city.

Judith: Chapter 7 Notes

1 Codex Vaticanus: Dôthaem (ⲆⲰⲐⲀⲓⲙ)

Dôthaem (Δωθαιμ) was the Greek transliteration of the Dosan (דֹּתָן), generally transliterated as Dothan with was also mentioned in Genesis chapter 37, and 2nd Kingdoms chapter 6. It is generally accepted as Tel Dothan (تل دوثان) in the northern region of the modern Palestinian West Bank, north of Nablus (نابلس), which was known as Shechem (שכם) at the time.

2 Codex Vaticanus: Belbaem (ⲃⲉⲗⲃⲀⲓⲙ)

3 Codex Vaticanus: Cyamônos (ⲕⲨⲀⲙⲰⲚⲟⲥ)

4 Codex Vaticanus: Egrebêl (ⲈⲄⲣⲉⲃⲏⲗ)

This name is accepted as being a reference to Aqraba (عقربا), in the Palestinian West Bank southeast of Nablus (نابلس), which was known as Shechem (שכם) at the time. The name of the town was very inconsistent in ancient literature. The Samaritan book of Joshua son of Nun, likely compiled in its current form circa 60 BC, records the name as Akrabith (ⵟⵎⵣⵏⴰⵢⵏ). The historian Josephus recorded the name as Acrabatta (Ακραβαττα) in Wars of the Jews from circa 70 AD.

In the Mishnah, composed circa 190 AD, the name was spelled as Aqrabat (אקראבאת). The pronunciation and spelling of the modern name Aqraba (عقربا) are derived from the Arabic word for scorpion (عقرب), however, this appears to be something that was adopted after the regions became predominantly Arabic speaking. The name in the Book of Judith appears to be much older as it translates as approximately 'Lord of Chance,' suggesting an older Canaanite name of the town: Akry-Ba'al (𐤋𐤏𐤁 𐤆𐤊𐤓𐤀).

5 Codex Vaticanus: Chous (ΧΟΥΣ)

6 Codex Vaticanus: Mochmour (ΜΟΧΜΟΥΡ)

Mochmour is a Greek transliteration of the name of the Mishmar (משמר), a river in southeast Israel. The translation is specific, however, the location is incorrect, as the river is nowhere near the towns listed. The correct river in the region is the Wady es-Suweinit in the Palestinian West Bank, which was known as the Michmas (מכמש) at the time. The Michmas was listed in Isaiah as being along the invasion route that Sennacherib took during his invasion during the reign of Hezekiah, which took place several decades earlier. It is unclear why the name would have been mistranslated as it was well known to the Library of Alexandria, and was previously translated correctly in 1st Kingdoms and Isaiah.

The only obvious reason for the substitution is that the Michmas was the base that the Maccabees were operating out of under Jonathan, during the Maccabean Revolt. If the translators chose to substitute the Mishmar for the Michmas due to political reasons, it means they almost certainly translated the text between 161 and 143 BC, when the Greeks still viewed the Maccabees as terrorists.

7 Codex Vaticanus: gên (ΓΗΝ). Translation: Ge (or earth, land)

Ge was the ancient Greek goddess of the Earth, who was used as the translation for Eretz (אֶרֶץ) in the Septuagint. Eretz was the Canaanite earth goddess.

8 Codex Vaticanus: theon hêmôn (ΘΕΟΝΗΜΩΝ). Translation: our god

9 Codex Vaticanus: cyrion tôn paterôn êmôn (ΚΥΡΙΟΝ ΤΩΝΠΑΤΕΡΩΝΗΜΩΝ). Translation: Lord of our fathers

Judith: Chapter 8

Now, at that time, Judith heard, who was the daughter of Merari ben Ox ben Joseph ben Oziel ben Elkiah ben Hananiah ben Gideon ben Raphaim ben Ahitub ben Elihu ben Hilkiah ben Eliab ben Nathanael ben Salamiel ben Sarasadae ben Israel. Her husband Manasseh, who was from her tribe and family, had died in the barley harvest. As he had stood overseeing those who bound sheaves in the field, the heat came on his head, and he fell to his bed and died in the city of Beit-illu. They buried him with his fathers in the field between Dothan and Balamon.[1]

Judith was a widow in her house for three years and four months. She pitched her a tent on the top of her house and wore sackcloth and her widow's apparel. She fasted all the days of her widowhood, other than the Friday, and Saturday, and the feasts of the New Moon, and the holidays of the house of Israel. She was also a friendly person, and very beautiful to look, and her husband Manasseh had left her gold and silver, and men-slaves and woman-slaves, and livestock, and lands, and she remained with them. No one said anything bad about her, for she was very afraid of God.

She heard the evil words of the people against their governor, and that they fainted for lack of water. Judith had listened to all the words that Uzziah had spoken to them, that he had sworn to deliver the city to the Assyrians after five days. Then she sent her chief servant woman, who administered all of her property to call Uzziah and Chabris and Charmis, the elders of the city.

They came to her, and she said to them, "Hear me now, you governors of Beitillu. The words that you have said to the people today are not right. This is an oath which you made, and pronounced between God and you, and have promised to deliver the city to our enemies unless within these days the Lord turns to help you. Now, who are you that have tempted God this day, and stand instead of God among the children of men? Brothers, you annoy the Lord God, but you will never know anything. You can't find the depth of the heart of man, or can perceive the things that he thinks, then how can you search out God who has made all these things, and know his mind or comprehend his purpose? No, my brothers, don't provoke the Lord God to anger. For if he will not help us within these five days, he has the power to defend us when he chooses or to destroy us before our enemies. Do not bind the counsels of the Lord God, for God is not as man that he can be threatened. Neither is he like the son of man, that he should be wavering. Therefore let us wait for salvation from him, and call on him to help us, and he will hear our voice if it pleases him."

"There have risen none in our age, neither is there any now in these days neither tribe, nor family, nor people, nor city among us, who worship gods made with hands, as it was before. It was the cause of our forefathers being given to the sword, and as plunder, and a great fell before our enemies. But we know no other god, therefore we trust that he will not hate us, or any of our nation. If we are captured, all Judah will lie waste and our temple will be spoiled, and he will require the profanation of at our mouth. The slaughter of our brothers, and the captivity of the country, and the desolation of our inheritance will he turn on our heads among the Gentiles, wherever we will be in slavery, and we will be an offense and an insult to all those who own us. For our slavery will not be directed to favor, but the Lord God will turn it to dishonor. Now, therefore, brothers, let us show an example to our brothers because their hearts depend on us, and the sanctuary, and the temple, and the altar rest on us. Moreover, let us give thanks to the Lord God, who tries us, even as he did our fathers. Remember the things he did to Abraham, and how he tried Isaac, and what happened to Jacob in Mesopotamia in Syria, when he kept the sheep of Laban his mother's brother? For he has not tried us in the fire, as he did them, for the examination of their hearts, neither has he taken vengeance on us, but the Lord does scourge those who come near to him, to admonish them."

Then Uzziah replied to her, "All you have spoken, you have spoken with a good heart, and there is none that may doubt your words. For this is not the first day in which your wisdom is has shown itself, but from the beginning of your days, all the people have known your understanding, because the disposition of your heart is good. But the people are very thirsty and compelled us to do for them as we have said and to bring an oath on ourselves which we will not break. Therefore now beg for us, because you are a godly woman, and the Lord will send us rain to fill our cisterns, and we will faint no more."

Then Judith replied to them, "Hear me and I will do something, which will be retold to all generations of the children of our nation. You will stand this night at the gate, and I will go out with my woman-servant, and within the days that you have promised to deliver the city to our enemies the Lord will visit Israel by my hand. But don't ask what I'm planing, as I will not tell you until I'm finished what I plan to do."

Uzziah and the princes said to her, "Go in peace, and the god the Lord be before you, to take vengeance on our enemies," and they returned from the tent, and went to their homes.

Judith: Chapter 8 Notes

1 Codex Vaticanus: Balamôn (ΒΑΛΑΜΩΝ)

The location of the village is unknown, however, the name of the village appears to have been Ba'al-Amen (𐤏𐤋 𐤀𐤌𐤍) in the Canaanite script that was in use at the time.

Judith: Chapter 9

Judith fell to her face, and put ashes on her head, and uncovered the sackcloth she was clothed in, and about the time that the incense of the evening was offered in Jerusalem in the Temple of the Lord, Judith cried with a loud voice, and said, "The Lord God of my father Simeon, to whom you gave a sword to take vengeance of the foreigners who loosened the girdle of a girl to rape her, and discovered the thigh to her shame, and polluted her virginity to her reproach, as you said, 'It will not be so,' and yet they did so. Therefore you gave their rulers to be slain, so that they died their bed in blood, being deceived, and slaughtered the servants with their lords, and the lords on their thrones, and took their wives as victims, and their daughters to be slaves, and all their spoils to be divided among your dear children, who were moved with your zeal, and abhorred the filth of their blood, and called on you for aid."

"God, my god, hear me also a widow. For you have worked not only those things, but also the things which happened before, and which continue after. You have thought about the things which are now, and which are to come. Yes, what things you did determine were ready at hand, and said, 'Look, we are here,' for all your ways are prepared, and your judgments are in your fore-knowledge. For, look, the Assyrians are multiplied in their power, they are exalted with horse and man, they glory in the strength of their infantry, they trust in shield, spear, bow, and sling, and don't know that you are the Lord who breaks the battles! Lord[1] is your name. Knock down their strength with your power, and bring down their force in your anger, for they have purposed to defile your sanctuary, and to pollute the tabernacle where your glorious name rests and to throw down with sword the horn of your altar. See their pride, and send your anger on their heads!"

"Give into my hand the power that I have conceived. Strike by the deceit of my lips the servant with the prince, and the prince with the servant. Break down their stateliness by the hand of a woman. For your power stands not in multitudes or your might in strong men. You are a god of the afflicted, a helper of the oppressed, an upholder of the weak, a protector of the forlorn, a savior of those who are without hope. I beg you, I beg you, God of my father, and God of the inheritance of Israel, ruler of the heavens and earth, creator of the waters, king of every creature, hear my prayer! Make my speech and deceit to be their wound and stripe, who intend cruel things against your covenant, and your sacred temple, and Mount Zion, and the house of the possession of your children. Make every nation and tribe to acknowledge that you are the god of all power and might and that there is none other that protects the people of Israel but you."

Judith: Chapter 9 Notes

1 Codex Vaticanus: cyrios (ΚΥΡΙΟϹ)

The Greeks translated the Aramaic words Adonai (ᴧϟϞℵ) and Ba'al (ℵℓᵛϽ) as 'lord' (κύριος). As this the term Adonai was used in the Aramaic sections of Daniel, Adonai is restored in the restoration.

Judith: Chapter 10

After that, she stopped praying to the god in Israel, and rose where she had fallen down, and called her girl, and went down into the house in the which she lived on the sabbath days, and in her feast days, and pulled off the sackcloth which she had on, and took off the garments of her widowhood, and washed her body all over with water, and anointed herself with precious ointment, and braided the hair of her head, and put on a tire on it, and put on her garments of gladness, where she was clad during the life of Manasseh her husband.

She put sandals on her feet and put around her bracelets, and her chains, and her rings, and her earrings, and all her ornaments, and decked herself bravely, to allure the eyes of all men that should see her. Then she gave her girl a bottle of wine, and a jar of oil, and filled a bag with parched grain, and lumps of figs, and with fine bread, so she folded all these things together, and loaded them on her. They went out to the gate of the city of Beitillu like this and found standing there Uzziah and the elders of the city, Chabris, and Charmis. When they saw her, that her look was altered, and her apparel was changed, they wondered at her beauty greatly and said to her, "The Lord God of our fathers give you favor, and accomplish your plans to the glory of the Israelites, and to the exaltation of Jerusalem."

Then they worshiped God, and she said to them, "Command the gates of the city to be opened from me, that I may go out to accomplish the things which we have spoken of."

They commanded the young men to open the gate for her, as she had asked, and when they had done so, Judith went out along with her girl, and the men of the city watched her until she had gone down the mountain and had passed out of the valley, and they could see her no more. They went straight out into the valley, and the first watch of the Assyrians met her, captured her, and asked, "Of what people are you? Where have you come from, and where are you going?"

She answered, "I am a Hebrew woman, and had fled from them, for they will be given you to be slaughtered. I am traveling to Holofernes the chief captain of your army, to declare words of truth, and I will show him a path, where he can go and win all the hill country, without the life of even one of his men."

When the men heard her words and saw her countenance, they wondered greatly at her beauty, and said to her, "You have saved your life, in that you have rushed to come down to the presence of our lord. Now, therefore come to his tent, and some of us will escort you until they have delivered you to his hands. When you stand before him, do not be afraid in your heart, but tell him as you have said, and he will treat you well."

They chose out from them a hundred men to accompany her and her girl, and they took her to the tent of Holofernes. Then was there a discussion throughout all the camp, as her coming was noticed among the tents, and they came out around her as she stood outside the tent of Holofernes, until they told him of her. They wondered at her beauty, and admired the Israelites because of her, and said to each other, "Who would despise these people, that have among them, such women? Certainly, it is not good that one man of them be left who being let go might deceive the whole earth."

They that camped near Holofernes went out, and all his servants and they brought her into the tent. Now Holofernes rested on his bed under a canopy, which was woven with purple, and gold, and emeralds, and precious stones. So they showed him of her, and he came out before his tent with silver lamps going before him. When Judith had come before him and his servants they all marveled at the beauty of her countenance, and she fell on her face and did reverence to him, and his servants picked her up.

Judith: Chapter 11

Holofernes said to her, "Woman, be of good comfort, don't be afraid in your heart, for I never hurt any that was willing to serve Nebuchadnezzar, the king of all the earth. Now, therefore, if your people that dwell in the mountains had not prepared to battle me, I would not have lifted my spear against them, but they have done these things to themselves. But now tell me why you have fled from them, and have come to us, for you have come to safety. Be of good comfort, you will live this night, and from now on, for none will hurt you, but treat you well as they do the servants of king Nebuchadnezzar my lord."

Then Judith said to him, "Hear the words of your servant and allow your slave-woman to speak in your presence, and I will not lie to my lord this night. If you will follow the words of your slave-woman, God will bring the thing perfectly to pass for you, and my lord will not fail of his purposes. As Nebuchadnezzar king of all the earth lives, and as his power lives, who has sent you for the upholding of every living thing, for not only men will serve him by you, but also the beasts of the field, and the livestock, and the birds of the air, will live by your power under Nebuchadnezzar and all his house. For we have heard of your wisdom and your policies, and it is reported in all the earth, that you only are excellent in all the kingdom, and mighty in knowledge, and wonderful in feats of war. Now as concerning the matter, which Achior spoke in your council, we have heard his words, for the men of Beitillu saved him, and he told them all that he had said to you."

"Therefore, lord and governor, don't reject his word, but take it up in your heart, for it is true. Our nation will not be punished, neither can sword prevail against them, except if they sin against their god. Now, my lord, do not be defeated and frustrate of purpose, even death has now fallen on them, and their sin has overtaken them, where they will provoke their god to anger when they will do that which is not to be done. For their food fail them, and all their water is almost gone, and they have determined to lay hands on their livestock, to consume all those things that God has forbidden them to eat by his laws. They have resolved to spend the first-fruits of the tenths of wine and oil, which they had sanctified, and reserved for the priests that serve in Jerusalem before the face of our god, the which things it is not lawful for any of the people so much as to touch with their hands. For they have sent some to Jerusalem, because they also that live there have done the like, to bring them permission from the senate."

"Now when they will bring them word, they will immediately do it, and they will be given to you to be destroyed the same day. Therefore I, your slave-woman, knowing all this have fled from their presence, and God has sent me to work things with you, where all the earth will be astonished, whoever will hear it. For your servant is religious and serves the god Shamayim, both day and night. Now, therefore, my lord, I will remain with you, and your servant will go out by night into the valley, and I will pray to God, and he will tell me when they have committed their sins. I will come and show it to you, then you will go out with all your army, and there will be none of those who will resist you. I will lead you through the middle of Judah until you come to Jerusalem, and I will set your throne in the middle of it, and you will drive them like sheep that have no shepherd, and a dog will not so much as open his mouth at you. These things were shown me through prophecy, and they were declared to me, and I am sent to tell you."

Her words pleased Holofernes and all his servants, and they marveled at her wisdom, and said, "There is not such a woman from one end of the earth to the other, both for the beauty of face, and wisdom of words."

Holofernes said to her, "God has done well to send you before the people, that strength might be in our hands and destruction on those who lightly regard my lord. Now you are both beautiful in your countenance, and witty in your words. Certainly, if you do as you have spoken your god will be my god, and you will live in

the house of king Nebuchadnezzar, and will be
renowned through the whole earth."

Judith: Chapter 12

Then he commanded to bring her in, to where his meal was set and commanded that they should prepare for her from his meats and that she should drink of his wine.

Judith said, "I will not eat of it, in case there be an offense, but provisions will be made for me of the things that I have brought."

Then Holofernes said to her, "If your provisions should run out, what should we give you? There are none with us from your nation."

Judith answered him, "As your soul lives, my lord, your slave-woman will not finish those things that I have brought before the Lord works by my hand the things that he has determined."

Then the servants of Holofernes brought her into the tent, and she slept till midnight, and she arose when it was towards the morning watch, and sent to Holofernes, saying, "Let my lord now command that your handmaid may go out to prayer."

Then Holofernes commanded his guard that they should not stop her, and so she lived in the camp three days, and went out in the night into the valley of Beit-illu, and washed in a fountain of water by the camp. When she came out, she implored the Lord God in Israel to direct her way to the salvation of the children of her people. She came in clean and remained in the tent until she ate her meat in the evening.

On the fourth day, Holofernes made a feast for his own servants only and called none of the officers to the banquet. Then said he to Bagoas the eunuch, who had command over all that he had, "Go and persuade this Hebrew woman which is with you, that she comes to us, and eats and drinks with us. For it will be a shame for us if we let such a woman go not having had her company, for if we do not have her, she will laugh us to scorn."

Then Bagoas left Holofernes and went to her, and he said, "Don't let this fair girl fear to come to my lord, and to be honored in his presence, and drink wine, and be merry with us and be made this day as one of the daughters of the Assyrians, which serve in the house of Nebuchadnezzar."

Then Judith said to him, "Who am I now, that I should not obey my lord? Certainly, whatever pleases him, I will do quickly, and it will be my joy until the day of my death."

She rose and clothed herself within her best woman's attire, and her girl laid soft skins on the ground for her near Holofernes, which she had received from Bagoas for her daily use, that she might sit and eat on them. Now when Judith came in and sat down, Holofernes's heart was ravished with her, and his mind was moved, and he greatly desired her company, as he had waited a time to deceive her from the day that he had seen her. Then Holofernes said to her, "Drink now, and celebrate with us."

Judith replied, "I will drink now, my lord, because my life is magnified in me this day more than all the days since I was born."

She took and ate and drank before him what her maid had prepared. Holofernes took great delight in her and drank more wine than he had drunk at any time in one day since he was born.

Judith: Chapter 13

When the evening had come, his servants rushed to leave, and Bagoas shut his tent outside and dismissed the waiters from the presence of his lord, and they went to their beds, for they were all tired, because the feast had been long. Judith was left alone in the tent with Holofernes lying along on his bed, for he was drunk with wine. Judith had commanded her slave-girl to stand outside her bedroom and to wait for her to come out as she did daily, for she said she would go out to her prayers, and she told Bagoas the same reason.

So all left and none were left in the bedroom, neither minor nor great. Then Judith, standing by his bed, said in her heart, 'Lord the god of all forces,[1] look at this present from the works of my hands for the exaltation of Jerusalem. For now is the time to help your inheritance, and to execute your enterprises to the destruction of the enemies which have risen against us.' Then she came to the pillar of the bed, where Holofernes's head was with his sword, approached his bed, and took hold of the hair of his head, and said, "Strengthen me today, Lord God of Israel!"

She slashed twice across his neck with all her might, and she pulled his head away from his body, and tumbled his body down from the bed, and pulled down the canopy from the pillars, and after she went out, and gave Holofernes his head to her slave-girl. She put it in her bag of meat, and they both went together according to their custom to prayer, and when they left the camp, they circled the valley, and went up the mountain of Beitillu, and came to its gates.

Then Judith shouted to the watchmen at the gate, "Open, open the gate now! God, our God, is with us! He has shown his power is still in Jerusalem, and his forces are against the enemy, as he has done this today!"

Now, when the men of her city heard her voice, they hurried to go down to the gate of their city, and they called the elders of the city. Then they all ran together, both small and great, as it was strange to those who she had returned. They opened the gate, and let them in, and made a fire for a light, and stood around them. Then she said to them with a loud voice, "Praise! Praise God! Praise God, I say, for he has not taken away his mercy from the house of Israel, but has destroyed our enemies by my hands this night!"

She took the head out of the bag, and showed it, and said to them, "Look! The head of Holofernes, the chief captain of the Assyrian army, and look the canopy, in which he laid in his drunkenness! The Lord has struck him by the hand of a woman! As the Lord lives, who has protected me while I traveled, my countenance has deceived him to his destruction, and yet he did not commit sin with me, defiling and shaming me."

All the people were wonderfully astonished, and bowed themselves and worshiped God, and said with one voice, "Blessed are you, our god, who has today brought to nothing the enemies of your people."

Then Uzziah said to her, "Daughter, blessed are you of the Highest God above all the women on the earth, and blessed be the Lord God who has created the heavens and the earth, who has directed you to the cutting off of the head of the chief of our enemies. For this, your confidence will not be forgotten from the heart of men, who remember the power of God forever. God turned these things to you for a perpetual praise, to visit you in good things because you have not spared your life for the affliction of our nation, but have revenged our ruin, walking a straight way before our God."

All the people said, "So be it, so be it."[2]

Judith: Chapter 13 Notes

1 Codex Vaticanus: Cyrie o theos pasês dynameôs (ΚΥΡΙΕ Ο ΘΕΟC ΠΑΛCΗC ΔΥΝΑΜΕΩC). Translation: Lord the god of all forces

The translation of dynameôs (δυνάμεως) was used as a translation of ṣbå (צבא) after Judea became independent under the Hasmonean Dynasty in 140 BC, indicating that the Septuagint's book of Judith was probably translated between 140 and 132 BC. In Aramaic, the language which was spoken in Judea during the Persian and Greek eras, ådny ṣbå (ΝℲℾ ℮ΥΥΝ) meant 'lord of desires,' which was later translated as 'Dionysus' in the Greek era. When the Hasmonean Dynasty seized control of Judea, they standardized the meaning of the word to ṣbå (צָבָא) 'military' or 'army,' making the Lord of Desires into the Lord of Wr in the newly standardized Hebrew language. As the Aramaic text the Greeks translated has to have predated the Maccabean Revolt, the Aramaic text would have read 'Lord the god of all desires,' however, the later Hebrew interpretation would be 'Lord the god of all armies.'

2 Codex Vaticanus: genoeto (ΓΕΝΟΙΤΟ). Translation: Earth forbid

As the original text could not have used the Greek expression, the term amen is imported from other Masoretic books. If the Canaanite expression amen was not derived from the name of the supreme Egyptian god Amen's name during the Egyptian rule of Canaan when if first appeared in the texts, it's possible it was based on the Akkadian word for artist, åummānu (𒀀𒈬𒆜𒂖𒌋), however, this seems less likely than the name of the Egyptian creator god. According to Egyptologists, during the New Kingdom era, Amen (𒀭𒀀𒈠𒀭) is believed to have been pronounced as Åman. Earlier, during the Middle Kingdom the name was pronounced as Jaman, explaining the pronunciation of Benjamin, and later during the Nubian dynasty, the name was pronounced as Åmon, explaining the pronunciation of King Amon's name.

Judith: Chapter 14

Then Judith said to them, "Hear me now my brothers, take this head and hang it on the highest place along your walls. So as soon as the morning appears, and the sun comes out above the earth, everyone grab his weapons, and every valiant man go out of the city. Set a captain over them, as though you were going down into the plains towards the watchmen of the Assyrians, but don't go down. Then they will pick up their armor, and will go into their camp, and wake up the captains of the Assyrian army, and will run to the tent of Holofernes, but will not find him. Then fear will fall on them, and they will flee before you. So you, and all who inhabit the land of Israel will chase them, and overthrow them as they go. But before you do these things, call Achior the Ammonite to me that he may see and know he who hated the house of Israel, and who sent him to us, has died."

Then they called Achior out from the house of Uzziah, and when he had come and saw the head of Holofernes, held in a man's hand among the assembly of the people, he fell and fainted. When they had wakened him, he fell at Judith's feet and did reverenced to her, and said, "Blessed are you in all the tents of Judah, and in all nations, which hearing your name will be astonished. Now please, tell me all the things that you have done in these days."

Then Judith told him among the people all that she had done from the day that she went out until that hour she spoke to them. When she had stopped speaking, the people shouted with a loud voice and made a joyful noise in their city. When Achior had seen all that the god in Israel had done, he believed in God greatly, and circumcised the flesh of his foreskin, and was joined to the house of Israel to this day. As soon as the morning arose, they hanged the head of Holofernes on the wall, and every man took his weapons, and they went out by bands to the passages of the mountain. When the Assyrians saw them they sent to their leaders, which came to their captains and tribunes, and every one of their rulers. So they came to Holofernes's tent for him, because he had command of all, and said, "Wake now our lord, for the slaves have become bold and have come down against us to battle, so they may be destroyed."

Then Bagoas went in and knocked at the door of the tent, as he thought that he had slept with Judith. Because no one answered, he opened it, and went into the bedroom and found him thrown on the floor dead, and his head had been taken from him. Therefore he cried with a loud voice, and wept and sighed, and with a mighty cry tore his clothes. After, he went into the tent where Judith had stayed, and when he did not find her, he ran out to the people, and cried, "These slaves have dealt treacherously! One Hebrew woman has disgraced the house of king Nebuchadnezzar! Look, Holofernes lies on the ground without a head!"

When the captains of the Assyrian armies heard these words, they tore their coats and their minds were troubled, and there was a cry and a very great noise throughout the camp.

Judith: Chapter 15

When they that were in the tents heard, they were astonished at the thing that was done. Fear and trembling fell on them, so that no man dared stay in the sight of his neighbor, but rushed out altogether, they fled into every road across the plains and through the hill country. They that had camped in the mountains around Beitillu fled away. Then the Israelites, everyone that was a warrior among them, rushed out and attacked them. Uzziah sent messages to Baetomasthaem, Bebai, Chobai, Cola, and to all the lands of Israel, to tell them the things that were done, and that all should rush out against their enemies to slaughter them.

Now when the Israelites heard it, they all attacked them as one, and slaughtered them at Chobai. Likewise also they that came from Jerusalem, and from all the hill country, (for men had told them the things that were done in the camp of their enemies) and they that were in Gilead, and in Galilee, chased them with a great slaughter, until they were past the borders of Damascus. The survivors that lived at Beitillu, attacked the camp of the Assyrians, and plundered them, and became very wealthy. The Israelites that returned from the slaughter had that which remained, and the villages and the cities, that were in the mountains and the plain, got a great deal of plunder, for the multitude was very great.

Then Jehoiakim the high priest and the elders of the Israelites that lived in Jerusalem came to look at the good things that God had shown to Israel, and to see Judith and to salute her. When they came to her, they blessed her with one voice and said to her, "You are the praise of Jerusalem! You are the great glory of Israel! You are the great rejoicing of our nation! You have done all these things by your hand! You have done a great deal of good for Israel, and God is pleased with you! You will be blessed because of the Omnipotent Lord in the centuries of time."

All the people said, "Amen!"

The people plundered the camp over the space of thirty days, and they gave to Judith Holofernes tent, and all his plates, beds, vessels, and all his belongings, and she took it and laid it on her mule, and prepared her carts and laid them on it. Then all the women of Israel ran together to see her, and blessed her, and danced for her, and she took branches in her hand, and gave also to the women that were with her. They put a garland of olive on her and her slave-girl that was with her, and she went before all the people in the dance, leading all the women, and all the men of Israel followed in their armor with garlands, and with songs in their mouths.

Judith: Chapter 16

Then Judith began to sing this thanksgiving hymn in all Israel, and all the people sang after her this song of praise. Judith sang, "Begin with timbrels for my God! Sing to my lord with cymbals! Tune for him a new psalm! Exalt him and call on his name! For God breaks the battles, among the camps among the people he has delivered me out of the hands of those who persecuted me! Ashur[1] came out of the mountains from the north! He came with ten thousand in his army! The multitude of it stopped the rivers, and their cavalry covered the hills. He bragged that he would burn up my lands, and kill my young men with the sword, and dash the sucking children against the ground, and make my infants as a prey, and my virgins as plunder. But Lord Omnipotent has disappointed them by the hand of a noose!"

"For the mighty one did not fall by the young men, neither did the sons of Titans[2] strike him, or tall Gigantes[3] attack him, but Judith the daughter of Merari weakened him with the beauty of her countenance. For she took off the garment of her widowhood for the exaltation of those that were oppressed in Israel, and anointed her face with ointment, and bound her hair in a tie, and took a linen garment to deceive him. Her sandals ravished his eyes, her beauty took his mind prisoner, and the sword passed through his neck. The Persians quaked at her boldness, and the Medes were daunted at her hardiness. Then my afflicted shouted for joy, and my weak ones cried aloud, but they were astonished. These lifted their voices, but they were overthrown. The sons of the girls have pierced them through and wounded them as fugitives' children. They perished in the battle of the Lord."

"I will sing to the Lord a new song. Lord, you are great and glorious, wonderful in strength, and invincible. Let all creatures serve you, for you spoke, and they were made, you did send out your spirit, and it created them, and none can resist your voice. For the mountains will be moved from their foundations with the waters, the rocks will melt like wax at your presence, yet you are merciful to those who fear you. For all sacrifice is too little for a sweet savor to you, and all the fat is not sufficient for your burnt offering, but he that fears the Lord is great at all times. Woe to the nations that rise against my families! Lord Omnipotent will take vengeance against them in the day of judgment, in putting fire and worms in their flesh, and they will feel them, and cry forever."

When they entered Jerusalem, they worshiped the Lord, and as soon as the people were purified, they offered their burnt offerings, and their free offerings, and their gifts. Judith also dedicated all the property of

Holofernes, which the people had given her, and gave the canopy, which she had taken out of his bedroom, as a gift to the Lord. So the people continued celebrating in Jerusalem before the sanctuary for the space of three months and Judith remained with them. After this time everyone returned to his inheritance, and Judith went to Beitillu, and remained in her possession, and was in her time honorable in all the country. Many desired her, but none knew her all the days of her life after Manasseh her husband was dead, and was gathered to his people. But she increased more and more in honor, and became old in her husband's house, being a hundred and five years old, and set her slave-girl free. She died in Beitillu, and they buried her in the cave of her husband Manasseh. The house of Israel lamented her seven days, and before she died, she did distribute her goods to all those who were nearest of families to Manasseh her husband, and those who were the nearest of her families. None caused the Israelites to fear again in the days of Judith or a long time after her death.

Judith: Chapter 16 Notes

1 Codex Vaticanus: Assour (ᴀccoyp). Translation: Ashur

Ashur (𒀭𒈗𒆠) was the patron god of the city of Assur, and the Assyrian Empire.

2 Codex Vaticanus: uioe titanôn (ʏιοιτιτᴀνωɴ). Translation: sons of Titans

Based on the pairing of the Gigantes and the 'sons of Titans,' this was probably a translation of Nefilim (נְפִלִים) and 'sons of Elohim' (בְּנֵי הָאֱלֹהִים) found in Genesis, where they were translated as Gigantes and 'sons of god.' The Greek translators interpreted these beings as either the sons of God in Genesis, while the Masoretic Text calls them the sons of the elohim.

They were called ôyryn (ܥܝܪܝܢ) meaning 'watchers' or 'guardians' in the Books of Enoch, and Grigori (ⰃⰓⰋⰃⰑⰓⰋ) in the Secrets of Enoch, likely transliterated from the Greek egirô (ἐγείρω) meaning 'awaken.' Given the similarity of the stories and the connections to Mount Hermon, they were likely based on the older Akkadian Igigi (𒀭𒄿𒄄𒄄), a group of lesser gods that rebelled against the ruling ᵃⁿAnuna (𒀭𒀯𒈾). The name ᵃⁿAnuna translates as 'sons of ᵈᵉⁱᵗʸSky' in Akkadian, suggesting this term was ᵃⁿAnuna in Cuneiform, and the following mention of the Gigantes were the Igigi who rebelled against them.

The ᵃⁿAnuna were a group of ruling gods, conceptually similar to the Olympian gods of Greek mythology. Significant members of this group of gods include ᵃⁿEnki (𒀭𒂗𒆠) the god of earth (or soil), and ᵃⁿEnlil (𒀭𒂗𒆤) the god of spirit who made the first humans in Mesopotamian beliefs. They were also called the ᵃⁿAnunakene (✳╟↙◈⟨⟩⟨⟩⊠⊣), more commonly transliterated into English as Anunnaki, as they were described as being the 'children of An (the sky god) on Ki (the Earth).

3 Codex Vaticanus: gigantes (ΓΙΓΛΝΤΕϹ). Translation: giants

Based on the pairing of the Gigantes and the 'sons of Titans,' this was probably a translation of Nefilim (נְפִלִים) and 'sons of Elohim' (בְּנֵי הָאֱלֹהִים) found in Genesis, where they were translated as Gigantes and 'sons of god.' The Hebrew term is accepted as meaning 'fallen,' and, the term is likely related to the Aramaic name for the Orion constellation, Npylyå (ℵ^ʿℓ^⁊ϟ). The term nefilim (נְפִלִים) likely originated as a description of the Orionid meteor shower that happens each year, between October 2 and November 7, as the Earth passes through the debris left by Halley's Comet. Peaks of 70 meteors a minute have been recorded, and these meteors fall from the region of the sky where Orion's upstretched arm is located.

The region of the sky where the constellations Orion and Lepus are located was known as the asterism Sah (╏⊿⊠╏✶) in the religion of the Egyptian Old Kingdom, which represented Sah, the father of the gods. The Sumerian version of Sah was ᵃⁿAn (✳✳), who was also the father of the gods, and represented by the stars of Orion.

The name Greek name Orion (Ὠρίων) is derived from the Akkadian Cuneiform name Uru-An (⟨𒀭⟩), meaning 'Light of An,' as the early Greeks learned of the asterism from the Canaanites that had settled in Cyprus. As the Greeks neither translated nor transliterated the term Nephilim, it is unlikely it was in the Aramaic text they translated, suggesting whatever term they found in the text was either conceptually or phonetically similar to the Greek Gigas (Γίγας). A more detailed version of this story appears in the Books of Enoch, where the term was translated into Ge'ez as ôyryn (ዐይሩን) meaning 'watchers' or 'guardians'. A similar term, egirô (ἐγείρω) meaning 'awaken,' appears to have been used in the Greek translation of Secrets of Enoch, which was later transliterated into Old Slavonic as Grigori (ⰃⰓⰋⰃⰑⰓⰋ). This indicates the original term was likely something that meant 'watcher' and sounded like Gigas, and given the connections to Mount Hermon, the Orion constellation, and thereby the god An, and his children the [an]Anuna (𒀭𒈹𒂗𒆠), the original term in the Cuneiform text was almost certainly Igigi (𒉪𒅆𒅆).

The Igigi were described as being a group of lesser gods that rebelled against the rule of the [an]Anuna, which translates as 'sons of the [deity]Sky,' and their name was the homophone of the Akkadian word igigi (𒅆𒅆) meaning to 'observe and measure.'

Restoration: Chapter 1

In the twelfth year of the reign of Ashurbanipal,[1] who reigned from the great Assyrian city of Nineveh, and in the days of Phraortes,[2] who ruled over the Medes from Ecbatana, he built stone cut walls around Ecbatana from stones three cubits wide and six cubits long. He made the height of the wall seventy cubits, and the width fifty cubits, and set the towers for the gates a hundred cubits high, and the width of the foundation sixty cubits. He made the gates that raised, seventy cubits high and forty cubits wide, for his mighty armies of infantry to go out through in formation.

In those days King Ashurbanipal declared war against King Phraortes in the great plain, which is the plain in the region of Ray. There came against him all those that lived in the hill country, and by the Euphrates, Tigris, and Harpasos[3] rivers, and from the plain of Uruk the king of the Elamites, and a great many tribes of the Chaldeans assembled themselves to the battle.

Ashurbanipal, king of the Assyrians sent messengers to all that lived in Persia, and to all that lived to the west.

---

1 See note 1 on page 22.

2 See note 3 on page 24.

3 See note 7 on page 26.

To those that lived in Cilicia, Damascus, Lebanon, Anti-Lebanon, and to all that lived on the sea coast, to the nations of Carmel, Gilead, Galilee, and the great plain of Yizre'el, to all that were in Samaria and the cities beyond the Jordan to Jerusalem, and Bethany, Chelus, Kadesh, and the river of Egypt, and Tahpanhes, and Ramesses, and all the land of Goshen, beyond Tanis and Memphis, and to all the inhabitants of Egypt to the borders of Kush. But all the inhabitants of the land ignored the commandment of Ashurbanipal king of the Assyrians and they did not accompany him into the battle, as they were not afraid of him. He was viewed by them as standing alone, and they sent away his ambassadors in disgrace.

Therefore Ashurbanipal was very angry with all these countries, and swore by his throne and kingdom, that he would certainly be avenged on all the lands of Cilicia, Damascus, and Syria, and that he would kill with the sword all the inhabitants of the land of Moab, Amman, Judah, and Egypt to the borders of the two seas. He marched in battle formation with his strength against King Phraortes in the seventeenth year,[4] and he defeated him in battle, and he overthrew the power of Phraortes, and all his cavalry, and all his chariots. He became lord of his cities, and traveled to Ecbatana, and captured the towers, and spoiled the streets, and turned

---

4 See note 16 on page 32.

its beauty into shame. He also captured Phraortes in the mountains of Ray, and pierced him with his darts, and destroyed him completely that day. Afterward, he returned to Nineveh, with his company of sundry nations, a great multitude of soldiers, and he relaxed and celebrated, both he and his army for a hundred and twenty days.

Restoration: Chapter 2

In the eighteenth year, the twenty-second day of the first month, there was talk in the palace of King Ashurbanipal of the Assyrians that he should, as he had said, avenge himself on all the earth. So he called all his officers and nobles to him and covertly made plans to conquer the whole earth. They decreed to destroy all flesh that did not obey the commandments of his mouth.

When he had ended his counsel, Ashurbanipal, king of the Assyrians called Holofernes the chief captain of his army, who was second only to him, and said, "This, says the great king, the Lord of the whole earth: Look, you will go out from my presence, and take your men that are confident in their own strength, a hundred and twenty thousand infantry, and twelve thousand cavalry. You will go against all the western countries because they disobeyed my commandment. Tell them to prepare the earth and the water for, I am coming in my fury against them and the feet of my armies will cover the whole face of the earth, and my troops will plunder them. Their slain will fill their valleys and brooks, and the rivers will be filled with their dead until they overflow. I will take captives to the furthest parts of all the earth. You will go beforehand for me and capture all their lands, and if they will surrender themselves to you, you will keep them for me until the day of their punishment. But those that resist, don't spare them, slaughter them and plunder from them wherever you go. For as I live, and by the power of my kingdom, whatever I have spoken I will do by my hand. Make sure that you don't break any of the commandments of your lord, but accomplish them fully as I have commanded you."

Then Holofernes went out from the presence of his lord and called all the governors and captains, and the officers of the Assyrian army. He mustered the chosen men for the battle as his lord had commanded him, a hundred and twenty thousand infantry, and twelve thousand archers on horseback. He organized them into a great army and marshaled them for the war. He took camels and donkeys for their chariots in great numbers, and sheep and oxen and goats without counting for their provision, plenty of food for every man of the army, and a great deal of gold and silver out of the king's palace. Then he set out with his army to go in advance of King Ashurbanipal in the expedition, and to cover the face of the earth to the west with their chariots, and cavalry, and their elite infantry. A great number also from the sundry countries traveled with them like locusts, and like the sand of the earth, for the multitude was without number.

They went out of Nineveh three days' journey towards the plain of the Cilician Gates[5] and camped near the Cilician Gates in the mountains that are near upper Cilicia. Then he took all his army, his infantry, cavalry, and chariots, and went from there into the hill country, and destroyed Phrygia[6] and Lydia,[7] and he captured all the children of Rassis, and the Ishmaelites who were near the wilderness to the south of the land around the capital. Then he crossed over the Euphrates and traveled through Mesopotamia, and destroyed all the high cities that were on the river, and crossed when you are near the sea. He conquered the lands of Cilicia, and slaughtered all that resisted him, and came to the borders of Jaffa, which were to the south near Arabia. He surrounded all the Midianites and burnt their tents, and destroyed their sheepfolds.

Then he went down into the plain of Damascus in the time of wheat harvest, and burnt up all their fields, and destroyed their flocks and herds, also he attacked their cities, and completely devastated their countries, and slaughtered all their young men with the edge of the sword. The fear and dread of him fell on all the inhabi-

---

5 See note 1 on page 38.

6 See note 3 on page 38.

7 See note 4 on page 39.

tants of the sea lands which were in Sidon, and Tyre and those that lived on the rocks,[8] and Acre, and all that lived in Yavne, and those that lived in Ashdod, and Ashkelon were terrified of him.

---

8 See note 10 on page 43.

Restoration: Chapter 3

They sent ambassadors to him to request peace, saying, "Look, we the servants of Ashurbanipal the great king lie in front of you, use us as will be good in your sight. Look, our houses, and all our places, and all our fields of wheat, and flocks, and herds, and all the lodges of our tents lie in front of you, use them as it pleases you. Look, even our cities and the inhabitants of are your servants, come and deal with them as seems good to you."

So the men came to Holofernes and told him this. Then he came down towards the sea coast, along with his army, and set garrisons in the high cities, and took from them elite men for aid. They and all the country around received them with garlands, with dances, and with timbrels. Yet he tore down their frontiers and cut down their Asherah,[9] for he had decreed to destroy all the gods of the land, that all nations should worship only Ashurbanipal, and that all tongues and tribes should praise him as God.

Also, he came up against Yizre'el near Judah, just across the great ridge of Judah. He camped between Gibeon and Scythopolis, and there he waited a whole month, so he could assemble all the chariots of his army.

---

9 See note 1 on page 46.

Restoration: Chapter 4

Now the Israelites that lived in Judah, heard all that Holofernes, the chief captain of King Ashurbanipal of Assyria, had done to the nations, and in what manner he had plundered all their temples, and reduced them to nothing. Therefore, they were very afraid of him and were concerned for Jerusalem, and for the Temple of Lord God. They were newly returned from the captivity, and all the people of Judah were lately gathered together, and the vessels, and the altar, and the temple were sanctified after the profanation. Therefore, they sent messages to all the lands of Samaria, and the villages, and to the House of Horon, Belmen, Jericho, Hobah, Esora, and to the valley of Salem. They occupied all the hilltops and fortified the villages that were on them, and stored up food for the provision of war, for their fields were recently reaped.

Also, Jehoiakim the high priest, who was in those days in Jerusalem, wrote to those who lived in Beitillu, and Betomestham, which is near Yizre'el towards the open country, near to Dothan, ordering them to hold the roads through the hill country, for through them was the entrance into Judah, and it was easy to stop anyone that would come through because the passage was only wide enough for two men at the most. The Israelites did as Jehoiakim the high priest and the elders of all the people of Israel who lived in Jerusalem had commanded them. Then every man of Israel cried to God with great fervency, and with great vehemency, they humiliated their minds. They, and their wives and their children, and their livestock, and every foreigner and employee, and their slaves bought with money, put sackcloth on their loins. Every man and woman, and the little children, and the inhabitants of Jerusalem, fell before the temple, and threw ashes on their heads, and spread out their sackcloth before the face of the Lord. Also, they put sackcloth around the altar, and cried to the god in Israel, that he would not give their children to be slaughtered, and their wives as plunder, and the cities of their inheritance to destruction, and the sanctuary to profanation and reproach, and for the nations to rejoice at.

God heard their prayers, and looked on their concerns, for the people fasted many days in all Judah and Jerusalem before the sanctuary of the holy Lord Shaddai.[10] Jehoiakim the high priest, and all the priests that stood before the Lord, and those who served the Lord had their loins girded with sackcloth, and offered the daily burnt offerings, with the vows and free gifts of the people, and had ashes on their miters, and cried to the Lord with all their power, that he would look on all the houses of Israel graciously.

---

10 See note 2 on page 49.

Restoration: Chapter 5

When Holofernes, the chief captain of the armies of Assyria, heard that the Israelites had prepared for war, and had blocked the roads through the hill country, and had fortified all the hilltops and had laid impediments to his campaign in those countries, he was very angry and called all the princes of Moab, and the captains of Amman, and all the governors of the sea coast. He said to them, "Tell me now, you sons of Canaan, who are these people that dwell in the hill country? What are the cities that they inhabit, and how large are their armies? What is their power and strength, and what king rules over them, or captain of their army? Why have they determined not to come and meet me, like the inhabitants of the west?"

Then Achior, the captain of all the Ammanites said, "Let my lord now hear a word from the mouth of your servant, and I will declare to you the truth concerning these people, who dwell near you, and inhabit the hill countries, and no lie will come out of the mouth of your servant. These people are descended from the Chaldeans. They previously lived in Mesopotamia, but because they would not follow the gods of their fathers, who were in the land of Chaldea, they left the way of their ancestors and worshiped the god Shamayim, the god who they knew. They drove them out from before their gods, and they fled into Mesopotamia, and stayed there many days."

"Then their god commanded them to leave from the place where they stayed and to go into the land of Canaan, where they lived and were increased with gold and silver, and with a great deal of livestock. But when a famine covered all the land of Canaan, they went down into Egypt, and stayed there, while they were nourished, and became a great multitude there, so that one could not count their nation. Therefore, the king of Egypt rose up against them, and dealt cleverly with them, and brought them low with laboring in brickmaking and made them slaves. Then they cried to their god, and he struck all the land of Egypt with incurable plagues, so the Egyptians cast them out of their sight. God dried the Papyrus Sea before them, led them along the road to Sinai, and Kadesh-Barne, and drove out all that lived in the wilderness, so they lived in the land of the Amorites, and they slaughtered all of the people of Heshbon, and passed across the Jordan they possessed all the hill country."

"They drove out before them the Canaanites, Perizzites, Jebusites, Shechem, and all the Girgashites, and they lived in that country many days. While they did not sin before their god, they prospered, because the god that hates iniquity was with them. But when they departed from the way which he appointed them, they were destroyed in many terrible battles and were led captives into a land that was not theirs, and the Temple of God was torn to the ground, and their cities were taken by the enemies."

"Now they have returned to their god, and have come back from the places where they were scattered, and have possessed Jerusalem, where their sanctuary is, and are seated in the hill country, yet before it was desolate. Now, therefore, my lord and governor, if there is any error against these people, and they sin against their god, let us consider that this will be their ruin, and let us go up, and we will conquer them. But if there is no iniquity in their nation, let my lord now˙ pass by, in case their god defends them, and we become a reproach before all the world."

When Achior finished sayings this, all the people standing around the tent murmured, and the chief men of Holofernes and all that lived by the seaside and in Moab said that he should kill him. For they said, "We will not be afraid of the Israelites! Look it is a people that have no strength or will for a strong battle. Now, therefore, Lord Holofernes, we will go up, and they will be prey to be devoured by all your army."

Restoration: Chapter 6

When the argument among the men of the council ended, Holofernes the chief captain of the Assyrian army said to Achior, and before the Moabites and all the company of other nations, "Who are you, Achior? The mercenary of Ephraim? You have prophesied against us today, and have said that we should not make war with the people of Israel because their God will defend them? Who is a god other than Ashurbanipal? He will send his power and will destroy them from the face of the earth, and their god will not deliver them. We, his servants will destroy them to the last man, for they are not able to stop the power of our horses. With them we will tread them underfoot, and their mountains will be drunk with their blood, and their fields will be filled with their dead bodies, and their infantry will not be able to stand before us, for they will completely perish. So says King Ashurbanipal, lord of all the earth."

He said, "None of my words will be in vain. You, Achior, an employee of Ammon, who have spoken these words in the day of your iniquity, will see my face no more from this day until I take vengeance on this nation that came out of Egypt. Then the sword of my army and the multitude of those who serve me will slaughter you, and you will fall among their dead when I return. Now my servants will take you back into the hill country, and will send you to one of the cities of the passages. You will not perish until you are destroyed with them. If you convince yourself in your mind that they will be taken, don't be depressed, as I have spoken it, and none of my words will be in vain."

Then Holofernes commanded his servants that waited in his tent, to take Achior, and bring him to Beitillu, and deliver him into the hands of the Israelites. So his servants took him and brought him out of the camp into the plain, and they went from the middle of the plain into the hill country and came to the fountains that were under Beitillu. When the men of the city saw them, they picked up their weapons and went out of the city to the hilltops, and every man that used a sling kept them from coming up by slinging of stones against them. Nevertheless having sneaked to the foot of the hill, they bound Achior, and threw him down, and left him at the foot of the hill, and returned to their lord.

The Israelites descended from their city, and came to him, and untied him, and brought him to Beitillu, and presented him to the governors of the city, which were in those days Uzziah the son of Micha, of the tribe of Simeon, and Chabris the son of Othniel, and Charmis the son of Malchiel. They called together all the elders of the city, and all their youths ran together, and their women, to the assembly, and they set Achior among their people. Then Uzziah asked him what was done. He answered

and declared to them the words of the council of
Holofernes, and all the words that he had spoken among
the Assyrian princes, and what Holofernes had said
proudly against the house of Israel.

Then the people fell and worshiped God, and cried to
God. saying, "Lord God Shamayim, look at their pride,
and pity the low estate of our nation, and look on the face
of those that are sanctified to you this day."

Then they comforted Achior and praised him greatly.
Uzziah took him out of the assembly to his house and
made a feast to the elders, and they called on the god in
Israel all that night for help.

Restoration: Chapter 7

The next day, Holofernes commanded all his army, and his people who had come to serve him, that they should move their camp towards Beitillu, to capture the roads into the hill country, and to make war against the Israelites. They moved their camps that day, and the army was 170,000 infantry, and 12,000 cavalry, beside the baggage, and other men that were on foot among them in very great numbers. They camped in the valley near Beitillu, by the fountain, and they covered a wide area around Dothan to Belbaem and on to Cyamonos, which is near Yizre'el.

Now when the Israelites saw the multitude of them, they were greatly troubled, and said to each other, "These men will consume the face of the earth. The high mountains, and the valleys, and the hills are unable to carry their weight."

Then every man took up his weapons of war, and when they had started fires in their towers, they remained and watched all that night. But on the second day, Holofernes brought out all his cavalry in the sight of the Israelites which were in Beitillu, and viewed the passages up to the city, and went to the fountains of their waters, and took them, and set garrisons of soldiers at them, and he left to return to his people.

Then all the chiefs of the children of Esau and all the governors of the Moabites, and the captains of the sea coast came to him and said, "Let our lord now hear our word, that your army is not defeated, as these people of Israel do not trust in their spears, but in the height of the mountains in which they live, because it is not easy to come up to the tops of their mountains. Now, therefore, my lord, don't fight against them in battle formation, and not even one of your men will die. Remain in your camp, and keep all the men of your army, and let your servants take into their hands the fountain of water, which issues out of the foot of the mountain. All the inhabitants of Beitillu get their water there, so thirst will kill them, and they will give up their city. We and our people will go up to the nearby hilltops and will camp on them, to watch that none leave the city, so they and their wives and their children will be consumed with fire, and before the sword that comes against them, they will be slaughtered in the streets where they live. Thereby will you award them for their evil in rebelling, and not meeting you peaceably."

These words pleased Holofernes and all his servants, and he appointed them to do as they had suggested. So the camp of the Ammanites departed, and with them, five thousand of the Assyrians, and they camped in the valley and captured the waters and the fountains of the waters of the Israelites. Then the children of Esau went up with the children of Amman and camped in the hill country near Dothan, and they sent some of them towards the south, and towards the east near Aqraba, which is near to Chous, that is on the River Michmas, [11] and the rest of the army of the Assyrians camped in the plain and covered the surface of the whole land. Their tents and chariots were camped in great numbers.

Then the Israelites cried out to the Lord God because they were afraid of all the enemies that had surrounded them, and there was no way to escape them. For thirty-four days the armies of Assyria remained camped around them with their infantry, chariots, and cavalry so that all the water store ran low for the inhabitants of Beitillu. The cisterns were empty and they had not drunk their fill of water, as they were rationing it. Their young children were scared, and their women and young men fainted for thirst and fell down in the streets of the city, and by the passages of the gates, and there was no longer any strength in them.

Then all the people assembled to Uzziah, and to the chief of the city, both young men, and women, and children, and cried with a loud voice, and said before all the elders, "God judge between us and you, for you have

---

11 See note 6 on page 66.

done us great injury in that you have not sought peace with the Assyrians. For now, we have no helper, but God has sold us into their hands, that we should be thrown down before them with thirst and great destruction. Now, therefore, call them to you, and deliver the whole city for plunder to the people of Holofernes, and to all his army. For it is better for us to be plundered by them than to die of thirst! We will be his slaves so that our souls may live and not see the death of our infants before our eyes, or our wives, or our children. We take as a witness against you Shamayim and Eretz, and our god, and Lord of our fathers, who punishes us according to our sins and the sins of our fathers, that he does not, as we have said this day."

There was great weeping with one consent in the middle of the assembly, and they cried to the Lord God with a loud voice. Then Uzziah replied to them, "Brothers, be of good courage, let us endure five more days, during which time the Lord God may turn his mercy towards us, for he will not forsake us completely. If these days pass, and there comes no help for us, I will do according to your words."

He dispersed the people, everyone to their own posts, and they went to the walls and towers of their city and sent the women and children into their houses, and they were very depressed in the city.

Restoration: Chapter 8

Now, at that time, Judith heard, who was the daughter of Merari ben Ox ben Joseph ben Oziel ben Elkiah ben Hananiah ben Gideon ben Raphaim ben Ahitub ben Elihu ben Hilkiah ben Eliab ben Nathanael ben Salamiel ben Sarasadae ben Israel. Her husband Manasseh, who was from her tribe and family, had died in the barley harvest. As he had stood overseeing those who bound sheaves in the field, the heat came on his head, and he fell to his bed and died in the city of Beit-illu. They buried him with his fathers in the field between Dothan and Balamon.

Judith was a widow in her house for three years and four months. She pitched her tent on the top of her house and wore sackcloth and her widow's apparel. She fasted all the days of her widowhood, other than the Friday, and Saturday, and the feasts of the New Moon, and the holidays of the house of Israel. She was also a friendly person, and very beautiful to see, and her husband Manasseh had left her gold and silver, and men-slaves and woman-slaves, and livestock, and lands, and she remained with them. No one said anything bad about her, for she was very afraid of God.

She heard the evil words of the people against their governor, and that they fainted for lack of water. Judith had listened to all the words that Uzziah had said to them, that he had sworn to deliver the city to the Assyrians after five days. Then she sent her chief servant woman, who administered all of her property to call Uzziah and Chabris and Charmis, the elders of the city.

They came to her, and she said to them, "Hear me now, you governors of Beitillu. The words that you have said to the people today are not right. This is an oath which you made, and pronounced between God and you, and have promised to deliver the city to our enemies unless within these days the Lord turns to help you. Now, who are you that have tempted God this day, and stand instead of God among the children of men? Brothers, you annoy the Lord God, but you will never know anything. If you can't find the depth of the heart of man, or can perceive the things that he thinks, then how can you search out God who has made all these things, and know his mind or comprehend his purpose? No, my brothers, don't provoke the Lord God to anger. For if he will not help us within these five days, he has the power to defend us when he chooses or to destroy us before our enemies. Do not bind the counsels of the Lord God, for God is not as man that he can be threatened. Neither is he like the son of man, that he should be wavering. Therefore let us wait for salvation from him, and call on him to help us, and he will hear our voice if it pleases him."

"There have risen none in our age, neither is there any now in these days neither tribe, nor family, nor people, nor city among us, who worship gods made with hands, as it was before. It was the cause of our forefathers being given to the sword, and as plunder, and a great many fell before our enemies. But we know no other god, therefore we trust that he will not hate us, or any of our nation. If we are captured, all Judah will lie waste and our temple will be spoiled, and he will require the profanation of at our mouth. The slaughter of our brothers, and the captivity of the country, and the desolation of our inheritance will he turn on our heads among the nations, wherever we will be in slavery, and we will be an offense and an insult to all those who own us. For our slavery will not be directed to favor, but the Lord God will turn it to dishonor. Now, therefore, brothers, let us show an example to our brothers because their hearts depend on us, and the sanctuary, and the temple, and the altar rest on us. Moreover, let us give thanks to the Lord God, who tries us, even as he did our fathers. Remember the things he did to Abraham, and how he tested Isaac, and what happened to Jacob in Mesopotamia in Syria, when he kept the sheep of Laban his mother's brother? For he has not tested us in the fire, as he did them, for the examination of their hearts, neither has he taken vengeance on us, but the Lord does scourge those who come near to him, to admonish them."

Then Uzziah replied to her, "All you have said, you have spoken with a good heart, and there is none that may doubt your words. For this is not the first day in which your wisdom has shown itself, but from the beginning of your days, all the people have known your understanding, because the disposition of your heart is good. But the people are very thirsty and compelled us to do for them as we have said and to bring an oath on ourselves which we will not break. Therefore now beg for us, because you are a godly woman, and the Lord will send us rain to fill our cisterns, and we will faint no more."

Then Judith replied to them, "Hear me and I will do something, which will be retold to all generations of the children of our nation. You will stand this night at the gate, and I will go out with my woman-servant, and within the days that you have promised to deliver the city to our enemies the Lord will visit Israel by my hand. But don't ask what I'm planning, as I will not tell you until I'm finished what I plan to do."

Uzziah and the princes said to her, "Go in peace, and the Lord the god be before you, to take vengeance on our enemies," and they returned from the tent, and went to their homes.

Restoration: Chapter 9

Judith fell to her face, and put ashes on her head, and uncovered the sackcloth she was clothed in, and about the time that the incense of the evening was offered in Jerusalem in the Temple of the Lord, Judith cried with a loud voice, and said, "The Lord God of my father Simeon, to whom you gave a sword to take vengeance of the foreigners who loosened the girdle of a girl to rape her, and discovered the thigh to her shame, and polluted her virginity to her reproach, as you said, 'It will not be so,' and yet they did so. Therefore, you gave their rulers to be killed, and they died in their beds in blood, after being tricked. The slaves were slaughtered with their owners, and the lords on their thrones. They took their wives as victims, and their daughters to be slaves. All their property was divided among your dear children, who were moved with your zeal, and abhorred the filth of their blood, and called on you for aid."

"God, my god, hear me also a widow. For you have worked not only those things, but also the things which happened before, and which continue after. You have thought about the things which are now, and which are to come. Yes, what things you did determine were ready at hand, and said, 'Look, we are here,' for all your ways are prepared, and your judgments are in your fore-knowledge. For, look, the Assyrians are multiplied in their power, they are exalted with horse and man, they glory in the strength of their infantry, they trust in shield, spear, bow, and sling, and don't know that you are the Lord who breaks the battles! Adonai[12] is your name. Knock down their strength with your power, and bring down their force in your anger, for they have purposed to defile your sanctuary, and to pollute the tabernacle where your glorious name rests and to throw down with sword the horn of your altar. See their pride, and send your anger on their heads!"

"Give into my hand the power that I have conceived. Strike by the deceit of my lips the servant with the prince, and the prince with the servant. Break down their stateliness by the hand of a woman. For your power stands not in multitudes or your might in strong men. You are a god of the afflicted, a helper of the oppressed, an upholder of the weak, a protector of the forlorn, a savior of those who are without hope. I beg you, I beg you, God of my father, and God of the inheritance of Israel, ruler of the heavens and earth, creator of the waters, king of every creature, hear my prayer! Make my speech and deceit to be their wound and stripe, who intend cruel things against your covenant, and your sacred temple, and Mount Zion, and the house of the possession of your children. Make every nation and tribe acknowledge that you are the god of all power

---

12 See note 1 on page 76.

and might and that there is none other that protects the people of Israel but you."

Restoration: Chapter 10

After that, she stopped praying to the god in Israel, and rose where she had kneeled down. She called her girl, and went down into the house in which she lived on the sabbath days, and in her feast days. She pulled off the sackcloth which she had on, and took off the garments of her widowhood, and washed her body all over with water, and anointed herself with precious ointment. She braided the hair of her head, and put a tiara on it, and put on her garments of celebration, which she had worn during the life of Manasseh her husband.

She put sandals on her feet and put around her bracelets, and her chains, and her rings, and her earrings, and all her ornaments. She decorated herself beautifully, to allure the eyes of all men that should see her. Then she gave her girl a bottle of wine, and a jar of oil, and filled a bag with parched grain, and lumps of figs, and with fine bread. She folded all these things together, and loaded them on her. They went out to the gate of the city of Beitillu like this and found standing there Uzziah and the elders of the city, Chabris, and Charmis. When they saw her, that her look was changed, and her clothes were changed, they wondered at her beauty greatly and said to her, "Lord the god of our fathers give you favor, and accomplish your plans to the glory of the Israelites, and to the exaltation of Jerusalem."

Then they worshiped God, and she said to them, "Command the gates of the city to be opened for me, that I may go out to accomplish the things which we have spoken of."

They ordered the young men to open the gate for her, as she had asked, and when they had done so, Judith went out along with her girl, and the men of the city watched her until she had gone down the mountain and had passed out of the valley, and they could see her no more. They went straight out into the valley, and the first watch of the Assyrians met her, captured her, and asked, "Of what people are you? Where have you come from, and where are you going?"

She answered, "I am a Hebrew woman, and had fled from them, for they will be given you to be slaughtered. I am traveling to Holofernes the chief captain of your army, to declare words of truth, and I will show him a path, where he can go and win all the hill country, without the life of even one of his men."

When the men heard her words and saw her countenance, they wondered greatly at her beauty, and said to her, "You have saved your life, in that you have rushed to come down to the presence of our lord. Now, therefore come to his tent, and some of us will escort you until they have delivered you to his hands. When you stand before him, do not be afraid in your heart, but tell him as you have said, and he will treat you well."

They chose out from them a hundred men to accompany her and her girl, and they took her to the tent of Holofernes. Then there was a discussion throughout all the camp, as her coming was noticed among the tents, and they came out around her as she stood outside the tent of Holofernes, until they told him of her. They wondered at her beauty, and admired the Israelites because of her, and said to each other, "Who would despise these people, that have among them, such women? Certainly, it is not good that one man of them be left who being let go might deceive the whole earth."

They who camped near Holofernes went out, and all his servants and they brought her into the tent. Now Holofernes rested on his bed under a canopy, which was woven with purple, and gold, and emeralds, and precious stones. They told him of her, and he came out before his tent with silver lamps going before him. When Judith had come before him and his servants they all marveled at the beauty of her countenance, and she fell on her face and did reverence to him, and his servants lifted her up.

Restoration: Chapter 11

Holofernes said to her, "Woman, be of good comfort. Don't be afraid in your heart, for I never hurt any that was willing to serve Nebuchadnezzar, the king of all the earth. Now, therefore, if your people that dwell in the mountains had not prepared to battle me, I would not have lifted my spear against them, but they have done these things to themselves. But now tell me why you have fled from them, and have come to us, for you have come to safety. Be of good comfort, you will live this night, and from now on, for none will hurt you, but treat you well as they do the servants of king Nebuchadnezzar, my lord."

Then Judith said to him, "Hear the words of your servant and allow your slave-woman to speak in your presence, and I will not lie to my lord this night. If you will follow the words of your slave-woman, God will bring the thing perfectly to pass for you, and my lord will not fail in his purposes. As Nebuchadnezzar king of all the earth lives, and as his power lives, who has sent you for the upholding of every living thing, for not only men will serve him by you, but also the beasts of the field, and the livestock, and the birds of the air, will live by your power under Nebuchadnezzar and all his house. We have heard of your wisdom and your policies, and it is reported in all the earth, that only you are excellent in all the kingdom, and mighty in knowledge, and wonderful in feats of war. Now as concerning the matter, which Achior spoke in your council, we have heard his words, for the men of Beitillu saved him, and he told them all that he had said to you."

"Therefore, lord and governor, don't reject his word, but take it up in your heart, for it is true. Our nation will not be punished, neither can sword prevail against them, except if they sin against their god. Now, my lord, do not be defeated and frustrate in your purpose, even death has now fallen on them, and their sin has overtaken them, where they will provoke their god to anger when they will do that which is not to be done. Their food fails them, and all their water is almost gone, and they have determined to lay hands on their livestock, to consume all those things that God has forbidden them to eat by his laws. They have resolved to spend the firstfruits of the tenths of wine and oil, which they had sanctified, and reserved for the priests that serve in Jerusalem before the face of our god, the things which it is not lawful for any of the people so much as to touch with their hands. They have sent some to Jerusalem, because they who live there have also done the same, and brought them permission from the senate."

"Now when they will bring them word, they will immediately do it, and they will be given to you to be destroyed the same day. Therefore I, your slave-woman,

knowing all this have fled from their presence, and God
has sent me to work things with you, where all the
earth will be astonished, whoever will hear it. For your
servant is religious and serves the god Shamayim, both
day and night. Now, therefore, my lord, I will remain
with you, and your servant will go out by night into the
valley, and I will pray to God, and he will tell me when
they have committed their sins. I will come and show it
to you, then you will go out with all your army, and
there will be none of those who will resist you. I will
lead you through the middle of Judah until you come to
Jerusalem, and I will set your throne in the middle of it,
and you will drive them like sheep that have no shepherd, and a dog will not so much as open his mouth at
you. These things were shown me through prophecy,
and they were declared to me, and I am sent to tell you."

Her words pleased Holofernes and all his servants, and
they marveled at her wisdom, and said, "There is not
such a woman from one end of the earth to the other,
both for the beauty of face, and wisdom of words."

Holofernes said to her, "God has done well to send you
before the people, that strength might be in our hands
and destruction on those who lightly regard my lord.
Now you are both beautiful in your countenance, and
witty in your words. Certainly, if you do as you have
spoken your god will be my god, and you will live in

the house of king Nebuchadnezzar, and will be renowned through the whole earth."

Restoration: Chapter 12

Then he commanded to bring her in, to where his meal was set and commanded that they should prepare for her from his meats and that she should drink of his wine.

Judith said, "I will not eat of it, in case there be an offense, but provisions will be made for me of the things that I have brought."

Then Holofernes said to her, "If your provisions should run out, what should we give you? There are none with us from your nation."

Judith answered him, "As your soul lives, my lord, your slave-woman will not finish those things that I have brought before the Lord works by my hand the things that he has determined."

Then the servants of Holofernes brought her into the tent, and she slept till midnight, and she arose when it was towards the morning watch, and sent to Holofernes, saying, "Let my lord now command that your handmaid may go out to prayer."

Then Holofernes commanded his guard that they should not stop her, and so she lived in the camp three days, and went out in the night into the valley of Beit-illu, and washed in a fountain of water by the camp. When she came out, she implored the Lord God in Israel to direct her way to the salvation of the children of her people. She came in clean and remained in the tent until she ate her meat in the evening.

On the fourth day, Holofernes made a feast for his own servants only and called none of the officers to the banquet. Then said he to Bagoas the eunuch, who had command over all that he had, "Go and persuade this Hebrew woman which is with you, that she comes to us, and eats and drinks with us. For it will be a shame for us if we let such a woman go not having had her company, for if we do not have her, she will laugh us to scorn."

Then Bagoas left Holofernes and went to her, and he said, "Don't let this fair girl fear to come to my lord, and to be honored in his presence, and drink wine, and be merry with us and be made this day as one of the daughters of the Assyrians, which serve in the house of Nebuchadnezzar."

Then Judith said to him, "Who am I now, that I should not obey my lord? Certainly, whatever pleases him, I will do quickly, and it will be my joy until the day of my death."

She rose and clothed herself within her best woman's attire, and her girl laid soft skins on the ground for her near Holofernes, which she had received from Bagoas for her daily use, that she might sit and eat on them. Now when Judith came in and sat down, Holofernes's heart was ravished with her, and his mind was moved, and he greatly desired her company, as he had waited a time to deceive her from the day that he had seen her. Then Holofernes said to her, "Drink now, and celebrate with us."

Judith replied, "I will drink now, my lord, because my life is magnified in me this day more than all the days since I was born."

She took and ate and drank before him what her maid had prepared. Holofernes took great delight in her and drank more wine than he had drunk at any time in one day since he was born.

Restoration: Chapter 13

When the evening had come, his servants rushed to leave, and Bagoas shut his tent outside and dismissed the waiters from the presence of his lord, and they went to their beds, for they were all tired, because the feast had been long. Judith was left alone in the tent with Holofernes lying alone on his bed, for he was drunk with wine. Judith had commanded her slave-girl to stand outside her bedroom and to wait for her to come out as she did daily, for she said she would go out to her prayers, and she told Bagoas the same reason.

So all left and none were left in the bedroom, neither minor nor great. Then Judith, standing by his bed, said in her heart, 'Lord the god of all desires,[13] look at this present from the works of my hands for the exaltation of Jerusalem. For now is the time to help your inheritance, and to execute your enterprises to the destruction of the enemies which have risen against us.' Then she came to the pillar of the bed, where Holofernes's head was with his sword. She approached his bed, and took hold of the hair of his head, and said, "Strengthen me today, Lord the god of Israel!"

She slashed twice across his neck with all her might, and she pulled his head away from his body, and tumbled his body down from the bed, and pulled down

---

13 See note 1 on page 92.

the canopy from the pillars, and after she went out, and gave Holofernes' head to her slave-girl. She put it in her bag of food, and they both went together according to their custom to prayer, and when they left the camp, they circled the valley, and went up the mountain of Beitillu, and came to its gates.

Then Judith shouted to the watchmen at the gate, "Open, open the gate now! God, our God, is with us! He has shown his power is still in Jerusalem, and his forces are against the enemy, as he has done this today!"

Now, when the men of her city heard her voice, they hurried to go down to the gate of their city, and they called the elders of the city. Then they all ran together, both small and great, as it was strange to those who she had returned. They opened the gate, and let them in, and made a fire for a light, and stood around them. Then she said to them with a loud voice, "Praise, Praise God, Praise God, I say! He has not taken away his mercy from the house of Israel, but has destroyed our enemies by my hands this night!"

She took the head out of the bag, and showed it, and said to them, "Look! The head of Holofernes, the chief captain of the Assyrian army, and look the canopy, in which he laid in his drunkenness! The Lord has struck him by the hand of a woman! As the Lord lives, who has protected me while I traveled, my countenance has deceived him to his destruction, and yet he did not commit sin with me, defiling and shaming me."

All the people were wonderfully astonished, and bowed themselves and worshiped God, and said with one voice, "Blessed are you, our god, who has today brought to nothing the enemies of your people."

Then Uzziah said to her, "Daughter, blessed are you of the Highest God above all the women on the earth, and blessed is the Lord God who has created the heavens and the earth, who has directed you to the cutting off of the head of the chief of our enemies. For this, your confidence will not be forgotten from the heart of men, who will remember the power of God forever. God turned these things to you for a perpetual praise, to visit you in good things because you have not spared your life for the affliction of our nation, but have revenged our ruin, walking a straight way before our God."

All the people said, "Amen! Amen!"

Restoration: Chapter 14

Then Judith said to them, "Hear me now my brothers, take this head and hang it on the highest place along your walls. So as soon as the morning appears, and the sun comes out above the earth, everyone grab his weapons, and every valiant man go out of the city. Set a captain over them, as though you were going down into the plains towards the watchmen of the Assyrians, but don't go down. Then they will pick up their armor, and will go into their camp, and wake up the captains of the Assyrian army, and will run to the tent of Holofernes, but will not find him. Then fear will fall on them, and they will flee before you. So you, and all who inhabit the land of Israel will chase them, and overthrow them as they go. But before you do these things, call Achior the Ammonite to me that he may see and know he who hated the house of Israel, and who sent him to us, has died."

Then they called Achior out from the house of Uzziah, and when he had come and saw the head of Holofernes, held in a man's hand among the assembly of the people, he fell and fainted. When they had wakened him, he fell at Judith's feet and did reverenced to her, and said, "Blessed are you in all the tents of Judah, and in all nations, which hearing your name will be astonished. Now please, tell me all the things that you have done in these days."

Then Judith told him among the people all that she had done from the day that she went out until that hour she spoke to them. When she had stopped speaking, the people shouted with a loud voice and made a joyful noise in their city. When Achior had seen all that the god in Israel had done, he believed in God greatly, and circumcised the flesh of his foreskin, and was joined to the house of Israel to this day. As soon as the morning arose, they hanged the head of Holofernes on the wall, and every man took his weapons, and they went out by bands to the passages of the mountain. When the Assyrians saw them they sent to their leaders, which came to their captains and tribunes, and every one of their rulers. So they came to Holofernes's tent for him, because he had command of all, and said, "Wake now our lord, for the slaves have become bold and have come down against us to battle, so they may be destroyed."

Then Bagoas went in and knocked at the door of the tent, as he thought that he had slept with Judith. Because no one answered, he opened it, and went into the bedroom and found him thrown on the floor dead, and his head had been taken from him. Therefore he cried with a loud voice, and wept and sighed, and with a mighty cry tore his clothes. After, he went into the tent where Judith had stayed, and when he did not find her, he ran out to the people, and cried, "These slaves have dealt treacherously! One Hebrew woman has disgraced the house of king Ashurbanipal! Look, Holofernes lies on the ground without a head!"

When the captains of the Assyrian armies heard these words, they tore their coats and their minds were troubled, and there was a cry and a very great noise throughout the camp.

Restoration: Chapter 15

When they that were in the tents heard, they were astonished at the thing that was done. Fear and trembling fell on them, so that no man dared stay in the sight of his neighbor, but rushed out altogether, they fled into every road across the plains and through the hill country. They that had camped in the mountains around Beitillu fled away. Then the Israelites, everyone that was a warrior among them, rushed out and attacked them. Uzziah sent messages to Baetomasthaem, Bebai, Chobai, Cola, and to all the lands of Israel, to tell them the things that were done, and that all should rush out against their enemies to slaughter them.

Now when the Israelites heard it, they all attacked them as one, and slaughtered them at Chobai. Likewise also they that came from Jerusalem, and from all the hill country, (for men had told them the things that were done in the camp of their enemies) and they that were in Gilead, and in Galilee, chased them with a great slaughter, until they were past the borders of Damascus. The survivors that lived at Beitillu, attacked the camp of the Assyrians, and plundered them, and became very wealthy. The Israelites that returned from the slaughter had that which remained, and the villages and the cities, that were in the mountains and the plain, got a great deal of plunder, for the multitude was very great.

Then Jehoiakim the high priest and the elders of the Israelites that lived in Jerusalem came to look at the good things that God had shown to Israel, and to see Judith and to salute her. When they came to her, they blessed her with one voice and said to her, "You are the praise of Jerusalem! You are the great glory of Israel! You are the great rejoicing of our nation! You have done all these things by your hand! You have done a great deal of good for Israel, and God is pleased with you! Blessed are you of Lord Shadday in the centuries of time."

All the people said, "Amen!"

The people plundered the camp over the space of thirty days, and they gave to Judith Holofernes tent, and all his plates, beds, vessels, and all his belongings, and she took it and laid it on her mule, and prepared her carts and laid them on it. Then all the women of Israel ran together to see her, and blessed her, and danced for her, and she took branches in her hand, and gave also to the women that were with her. They put a garland of olive on her and her slave-girl that was with her, and she went before all the people in the dance, leading all the women, and all the men of Israel followed in their armor with garlands, and with songs in their mouths.

Restoration: Chapter 16

Then Judith began to sing this thanksgiving hymn in all Israel, and all the people sang after her this song of praise. Judith sang, "Begin with timbrels for my God! Sing to my lord with cymbals! Tune for him a new psalm! Exalt him and call on his name! For God breaks the battles, among the camps among the people he has delivered me out of the hands of those who persecuted me! Ashur came out of the mountains from the north! He came with ten thousand in his army! The multitude of it stopped the rivers, and their cavalry covered the hills. He bragged that he would burn up my lands, and kill my young men with the sword, and dash the sucking children against the ground, and make my infants as a prey, and my virgins as plunder. But Lord Shaddai has disappointed them by the hand of a noose!"

"For the mighty one did not fall by the young men, neither did the sons of Elohim[14] strike him, or tall Nephilim[15] attack him, but Judith the daughter of Merari weakened him with the beauty of her countenance. For she took off the garment of her widowhood for the exaltation of those that were oppressed in Israel, and anointed her face with ointment, and bound her hair in a tie, and took a linen garment to deceive him. Her sandals

---

14 See note 2 on page 104.

15 See note 3 on page 105.

ravished his eyes, her beauty took his mind prisoner, and the sword passed through his neck. The Persians quaked at her boldness, and the Medes were daunted at her hardiness. Then my afflicted shouted for joy, and my weak ones cried aloud, but they were astonished. These lifted their voices, but they were overthrown. The sons of the girls have pierced them through and wounded them as fugitives' children. They perished in the battle of the Lord."

"I will sing to the Lord a new song. Lord, you are great and glorious, wonderful in strength, and invincible. Let all creatures serve you, for you spoke, and they were made, you did send out your spirit, and it created them, and none can resist your voice. For the mountains will be moved from their foundations with the waters, the rocks will melt like wax at your presence, yet you are merciful to those who fear you. For all sacrifice is too little for a sweet savor to you, and all the fat is not sufficient for your burnt offering, but he that fears the Lord is great at all times. Woe to the nations that rise against my families! Omnipotent Lord will take vengeance against them in the day of judgment, in putting fire and worms in their flesh, and they will feel them, and cry forever."

When they entered Jerusalem, they worshiped the Lord, and as soon as the people were purified, they offered their burnt offerings, and their free offerings, and their gifts. Judith also dedicated all the property of Holofernes, which the people had given her, and gave the canopy, which she had taken out of his bedroom, as a gift to the Lord. So the people continued celebrating in Jerusalem before the sanctuary for the space of three months and Judith remained with them. After this time everyone returned to his inheritance, and Judith went to Beitillu, and remained in her possession, and was in her time honorable in all the country. Many desired her, but none knew her all the days of her life after Manasseh her husband was dead, and was gathered to his people. But she increased more and more in honor, and became old in her husband's house, being a hundred and five years old, and set her slave-girl free. She died in Beitillu, and they buried her in the cave of her husband Manasseh. The house of Israel lamented her seven days, and before she died, she did distribute her goods to all those who were nearest of families to Manasseh her husband, and those who were the nearest of her families. None caused the Israelites to fear again in the days of Judith or a long time after her death.

Septuagint Manuscripts

The following is a list of the Septuagint manuscripts referenced in the notes for this book.

LXX A (Codex Alexandrinus) is dated to the 5th century. It is currently located at the British Library (Royal 1 D. VIII) in London.

LXX B (Codex Vaticanus) is dated to the 4th century. It is currently located at the Vatican Library (Gr. 1209) in Vatican City.

Also Available

Also Available

- Octateuch: The Original Orit

ENOCH AND METATRON SERIES:
- Books of Enoch Collection

- Books of Enoch and Metatron Collection

- Books of Metatron Collection

- Secrets of Enoch

OTHER TRANSLATIONS:
- Apocalypses of Ezra

- Arabic Maccabees

- Life of Adam and Eve

- Memories of the New Kingdom

- Septuagint's Esther and the Vetus Latina Esther

- Septuagint's Ezekiel and the Ba'al Cycle

- Septuagint's Job and the Testament of Job

- Septuagint's Proverbs and the Wisdom of Amenemope

- The Amarna Letters

- Testaments of the Patriarchs Collection

- Tobit and Ahikar

- Ugaritic Texts: Ba'al Cycle

- Wisdom of Ahikar